AIRBNB MASTERY AND OPTIMIZATION 2-IN-1 BOOK

HOW TO SET UP AND RUN A SUCCESSFUL AIRBNB BUSINESS + HOW TO UNLEASH YOUR AIRBNB'S FULL POTENTIAL - FROM BEGINNER BASICS TO ADVANCED RENTAL TECHNIQUES

FRANK EBERSTADT

Copyright © 2022 Frank Eberstadt. All rights reserved.

The content contained within this book may not be reproduced, duplicated or transmitted without direct written permission from the author or the publisher.

Under no circumstances will any blame or legal responsibility be held against the publisher or author for any damages, reparation, or monetary loss due to the information contained within this book, either directly or indirectly.

Legal Notice:

This book is copyright protected. It is only for personal use. You cannot amend, distribute, sell, use, quote or paraphrase any part, or the content within this book, without the consent of the author or publisher.

Disclaimer Notice:

Please note the information contained within this document is for educational and entertainment purposes only. All effort has been executed to present accurate, up-to-date, reliable, complete information. No warranties of any kind are declared or implied. Readers acknowledge that the author is not engaged in the rendering of legal, financial, medical, or professional advice. The content within this book has been derived from various sources. Please consult a licensed professional before attempting any techniques outlined in this book.

By reading this document, the reader agrees that under no circumstances is the author responsible for any losses, direct or indirect, that are incurred as a result of the use of the information contained within this document, including, but not limited to, errors, omissions, or inaccuracies.

CONTENTS

HOW TO SET UP AND RUN A SUCCESSFUL AIRBNB BUSINESS

Introduction	13
1. AIRBNB BASICS	17
What Is Airbnb?	18
How It Works	20
Is Airbnb Safe?	22
2. DIFFERENT TYPES OF AIRBNB ACCOMMODATIONS	25
Four Main Types of Places Offered via Airbnb	25
Specialized Accommodations	26
3. THE TRUTH ABOUT AIRBNB HOSTING—MYTH VS. REALITY	33
Myth 1: The Vacation Rental Industry Is Sketchy	33
Myth 2: Being a Host Means You Can't Go Anywhere Else	34
Myth 3: Airbnb Is Only Profitable in the West	35
Myth 4: Airbnb Guests Are Mostly Party People Who Cause Trouble and Destroy Furniture	35
Myth 5: Becoming an Airbnb Host Is Only About Business	36
Myth 6: Airbnb Rentals Are Bad for My Neighborhood	37
4. 9 SIGNS STARTING AN AIRBNB BUSINESS IS RIGHT FOR YOU	39
Sign #1: You Have a Knack for Hospitality	39
Sign #2: The Market Conditions Are There	40
Sign #3: You're in It for More than Just a Quick Buck	40
Sign #4: You Have Enough Starting Capital	41
Sign #5: It's Actually Allowed in Your Jurisdiction	42

Sign #6: You Have Enough Time and Energy	42
Sign #7: You're OK with the Costs	43
Sign #8: You Have Enough Risk Tolerance	44
Sign #9: You Are Comfortable with Strangers in Your Home	44

5. THE "AIRBNB FRAMEWORK" FOR STARTING YOUR OWN SUCCESSFUL AIRBNB BUSINESS ... 47
The "Airbnb Framework" ... 47

Stage 1 ... 51
Analyzing the Market

6. HOW TO ANALYZE THE PLAYING FIELD ... 53
Tools You'll Need ... 53
Factors to Consider ... 56

7. PROS AND CONS OF RENTING OUT DIFFERENT PROPERTY TYPES ... 63
Different Types of Rental Properties ... 64

8. WHAT'S THE MOST PROFITABLE TYPE OF AIRBNB LISTING? ... 69
Calculating Profitability ... 69
Expenses by Accommodation Type ... 72

Stage 2 ... 77
Airbnb Insurance

9. AIRBNB INSURANCE—WHICH TYPE OF POLICY SHOULD YOU GET? ... 79
Airbnb Insurance: What Every Host Needs to Know ... 79

10. SAFETY TIPS FOR HOSTS ... 85
Most Common Problems That Hosts Face ... 85
Best Safety Practices for Airbnb Hosts ... 87

Stage 3 ... 93
Readying Your Property

11. THE ULTIMATE CHECKLIST FOR ITEMS TO BUY FOR YOUR PROPERTY ... 95
Bathroom(s) ... 95
Bedroom(s) ... 96

Kitchen	97
Living Room	97
Appliances	98
Safety Equipment	98
Cleaning Supplies and Equipment	98

12. TOP 10 TIPS FOR ESTABLISHING EFFECTIVE HOUSE RULES — 101
    What Are Airbnb's House Rules? — 101
    Top Tips for Setting House Rules — 102

13. HOW TO CREATE YOUR HOUSE MANUAL — 107
    What Is a House Manual? — 107
    What Does a House Manual Look Like? — 108

14. LEGAL REGULATIONS TO CONSIDER — 113
    Common Legal Restrictions Related to Airbnb — 113
    Where to Look for Applicable Laws and Regulations — 116

15. A CLEAN PROPERTY LEADS TO 5-STAR REVIEWS — 119
    Turning Over Your Property — 120
    Remember to Restock and Restage — 122
    Create a Checklist — 124

Stage 4 — 131
Setting Up and Managing Bookings

16. BOOKING POLICIES TO CONSIDER — 133
    Common Booking Policies That Guests Ask About — 133

17. THE PRICE IS RIGHT—STRATEGIES FOR MAXIMIZING PROFITS AND INCOME — 139
    How to Figure Out Your Airbnb Pricing Strategy — 139
    Effective Airbnb Pricing Strategies — 141
    Online Tools — 147

18. STREAMLINING THE BOOKING PROCESS—
    HOW TO FIND GREAT GUESTS 149
    What Is Instant Book? 149
    How to Screen Guests When They Instant Book 151
    Story Time 152

19. RENTAL CHANNEL MANAGERS 157
    What Is a Channel Manager? 157
    What to Look for in Channel Manager Software 158

    Stage 5 161
    Getting Noticed

20. HOW TO CREATE YOUR FIRST AIRBNB
    LISTING 163
    How to List on Airbnb 163
    Other Short-Term Rental Platforms 165

21. HOW TO OPTIMIZE YOUR LISTING TO
    MAXIMIZE BOOKINGS AND INCOME 169
    How to Rank on the First Page SEO 169

22. HOW TO CAPTURE ATTRACTIVE PHOTOS OF
    YOUR PROPERTY 175
    Getting a Professional vs. Shooting Your Own
    Photos 176
    Tips for Taking Amazing Pictures of Your
    Property 177

23. LISTING TITLES THAT GET CLICKS 181
    Secret Tips and Formulas for Writing Titles That
    Increase Bookings 182

24. WRITING LISTING DESCRIPTIONS THAT
    MAKE GUESTS INSTANTLY BOOK WITH YOU 185
    What Makes a Listing Description Effective? 185
    The Basic Structure of a Top-Performing
    Description 187
    An Example of High-Performing Descriptions 188

25. THE POWER OF WORD OF MOUTH—GETTING
    PROFITABLE REVIEWS 191
    Tips for Getting Top-Rated Reviews from Guests 191

Stage 6   199
Building Relationships with Your Guests

26. 20 ESSENTIAL QUALITIES OF EVERY SUCCESSFUL AIRBNB BUSINESS OWNER   201
    20 Qualities of Successful Airbnb Business Owners   201

27. WHEN AND HOW TO USE AUTOMATION FOR YOUR AIRBNB RENTAL   205
    The Benefits of Automating Your Airbnb Business   205

    Conclusion   211
    References   213
    Notes   221

HOW TO UNLEASH YOUR AIRBNB'S FULL POTENTIAL

Introduction   225

1. UNDERSTANDING THE MARKET   229
   Conducting Market Research   230
   Recognizing Peak Seasons and Events   233
   Connection with Local Tourism Operators and Businesses   234

2. STRATEGIC PRICING 101   237
   The Basics of Dynamic and Static Pricing   237
   General Pricing Guide   241
   Pricing Strategies for Different Property Types   242

3. ADVANCED PRICING STRATEGIES   245
   Strategies for Weekdays and Weekends   247
   Strategies for Orphan Days   248
   Strategies Based on Lead Time   249

4. TRANSITIONING AND DIVERSIFICATION   251
   Shifting from Short-Term Rentals (STR) to Mid-Term Rentals (MTR)   251
   Increasing Occupancy   256
   Additional Revenue Sources   260

5. DATA ANALYTICS AND METRICS   265
   The Power of Data Analytics   266
   Different Metrics to Track   268

6. OPTIMIZING YOUR AIRBNB LISTING   271
   Why a Completed Listing Matters   271
   Improving Title, Description, and Amenities   273
   Tips for Increasing Visibility in Search   275

7. BUILDING A STRONG REPUTATION   279
   Becoming a Superhost   280
   Collecting Five-Star Reviews   281
   Encouraging Repeat Guests   283

8. MASTERING GUEST COMMUNICATION   289
   Automating Guest Messages   289
   Check-In Options: In-Person or Remote   292
   Dealing with Problem Guests   295

9. AUTOMATION AND TIME MANAGEMENT   299
   Automating Rulesets   299
   Scheduling and Automating Guest Check-Ins   301
   Automating or Outsourcing Cleaning and
   Maintenance   304

10. FINANCIAL CONSIDERATIONS   309
    Choosing the Right Cancellation Policies   309
    Understanding the Additional Fees   312

11. INNOVATIVE STRATEGIES FOR BOOSTING
    BOOKINGS   319
    Switching to Per-Room Listing   320
    Pet-Friendly Properties   320
    Rental Arbitrage   323

12. RISK MANAGEMENT AND POLICIES   327
    Setting House Rules and Security Deposits   327
    Airbnb's AirCover   331

13. EXPANDING YOUR REACH ... 335
   Listing on Multiple OTAs and Creating a Direct
   Booking Site ... 335
   Using Social Media for Marketing ... 341
   Becoming a Co-Host for Other Airbnb Owners ... 347

14. CHOOSING THE RIGHT TOOLS FOR
    MANAGEMENT ... 351
    PMS and Pricing Managers ... 351
    Instant Book and Smart Pricing ... 354

   Conclusion ... 359
   References ... 361

   About the Author ... 369

HOW TO SET UP AND RUN A SUCCESSFUL AIRBNB BUSINESS

OUTEARN YOUR COMPETITION WITH SKYROCKETING RENTAL INCOME AND LEAVE YOUR 9 TO 5 JOB EVEN IF YOU ARE AN ABSOLUTE BEGINNER

INTRODUCTION

The longer you're not taking action the more money you're losing.

— CARRIE WILKERSON

Imagine a life in which you get to visit the most beautiful and interesting places in the world. Imagine meeting new people, visiting historic sites, hiking beautiful trails, and finding local treasures. People want to have these kinds of experiences. Back in my single days, I lived that life and saw parts of the world that others could only dream of visiting. Then, after marrying my amazing wife and starting a family, I got to share my travels with my wife and kids. You might be wondering how this was possible. The truth is, if it weren't for Airbnb, I wouldn't have had these experiences and been able to see the world in so many unique ways.

As a solo backpacker, you don't have much money for travel—the main goal is to see the world's amazing sights. You also want to meet people and experience culture by immersing yourself in it—you want to stay where all the action is. Then, when you trade this life in for growing a family, you have to be more conscious of the little ones. Vacations become more about spending time with your family and enjoying the immediate surroundings. While you might still have a few adventures here and there, the main goal is to connect with your family in a special place. Being an avid traveler in both stages of my life allowed me to stay in a variety of Airbnbs—I know what works and what doesn't.

If all the traveling adventures weren't enough, we decided to make a huge move that came with many challenges and so many beautiful memories. We picked up our lives and emigrated to the Land Down Under.

Shortly after arriving in Australia, I knew I wanted to be in the accommodation business—I started working for an investment group that operated hotels and motels. Alongside this, I established my own property business. You could say that I have a passion for property and travel. What better way to combine these two than with Airbnb?

If you are someone with the same interests, then Airbnb is definitely for you. It provides a unique opportunity to deliver a fantastic travel experience to other people. If you have traveled before, you will know what a huge difference accommodation can make. I know that, out of all my travels, the accommodations were the travel experiences that I enjoyed the most.

If there was anything I wanted to make money from, it would be through properties. I loved the industry, and I knew that so many other people did as well. Everybody wants a fantastic vacation. There are so many complexities when starting a business and building an additional income that you want to enjoy the process—this is why Airbnb is such a great opportunity. Hosting people is an absolute pleasure if you know how to do it right. Not only that but investing in property means you have future security. Not only will you make an income, but you will always have your property to fall back on if you ever need additional income or a place to stay—a terrific method for maximizing control over your finances and avoiding economic unpredictability.

Currently, I have six properties and still work for the investment group I mentioned earlier. I'm quite experienced in the real estate industry, and more importantly, I have an Airbnb business. Throughout my time in this industry, I've learned quite a few lessons, and I've had to do them independently. That is the more challenging option, but you don't have to take that route. The knowledge that has taken me twelve years to accumulate, I want to pass on to you so that you can build up your Airbnb business and have it run smoothly without going through all my ups and downs.

When you start an Airbnb business, you will be able to become financially stable and simultaneously enjoy the process. When you become an Airbnb host, you open your doors to the rest of the world. The types of people you meet, the experiences you will have, and the stories you will get to tell all add to the wealth-building you will be participating in. Developing an Airbnb business is an investment in a better future for you and your family. By now, you are probably itching to find out how you can step into this journey so let's dive straight into Chapter 1.

1

AIRBNB BASICS

Over 150 million users worldwide have booked over 1 billion stays using Airbnb[1]. That is a lot of people who are looking for a unique and convenient place to stay when they go away. The traveling market has opened up, and people are looking for more affordable places to stay when they are traveling. It is essential to understand the basics of Airbnb before you can move on and create a strategy that will help you tap into all the benefits that come with it.

WHAT IS AIRBNB?

In the simplest of terms, Airbnb is an alternative to hotels. It allows individual property owners to list and rent their properties or rooms via the platform. The average property owner has access to a whole list of new clients they would not have otherwise. It also allows guests to find new, interesting, and often, inexpensive options for their vacation, business, or other travel needs. Before, you would need to be a hotel or a large rental chain to get enough business. Now, any person who has an available property can rent it out and make additional income.

The origin story of Airbnb is quite interesting. To say that it was something intentional wouldn't be true. It all started in 2007 when Brian Chesky and Joe Gebbia were completely broke and looking to make some extra money.[2] They lived in an apartment in San Francisco and needed a way to help pay their rent. They discovered a conference happening in their area and decided to rent out an empty room with an air mattress in their apartment for some extra cash. They called the service "AirBed & Breakfast." As you can see, this is where the name originated. Over a few years, this small idea grew, with the help of Nathan Blecharczyk, into the Airbnb platform we know today.

It is easy to look at the company and think it was an easy ride. Everybody loves to travel, and doing it uniquely and cheaply makes sense, right? However, the conception of this idea was purely accidental. When they were trying to build up the company, people genuinely thought they were crazy. Very few people thought this would be a good idea that would be profitable in the future. If you look at it in the context of 2007 or 2008, who wants to pay money to stay on an air mattress? They struggled to get investors to buy into their idea.

While you can see things from the investors' point of view, the people booking with them were telling a different story. People were even sharing their resumes and LinkedIn profiles to show that they were responsible and not security risks. They wanted a unique spot to stay, and this was when the founders believed they were onto something. After a while, they were accepted into a start-up accelerator program in San Francisco called Y Combinator, one of the points where the company pivoted. The idea suddenly started to catch fire and gain traction.

Airbnb has opened up real estate investing to the general public. You can make some money even if you are a recent graduate with only a small property. You don't even have to own the property yourself. Many renters are able to utilize

Airbnb to make some extra money. It has opened up a whole new world for travel and for making extra money for yourself.

HOW IT WORKS

Airbnb is an interesting concept. One important thing that people often misunderstand is that the Airbnb platform does not own any of the properties that are advertised on the website. Most of the control is left up to the host. The host will decide if they are comfortable with the offer, the price, and many other aspects of their rental property. The Airbnb platform is simply the intermediary between the guest and the host. Some rules and regulations need to be followed to ensure that the guests have the best experience possible and the hosts are protected.

Guests

If you have stayed in an Airbnb before, you will probably understand how it works for a guest. It's a pretty straightforward process, and it's user-friendly. To utilize the platform as a guest, you just set up an account on the platform.

Once your profile is complete, you can scroll through the listings until you find a property you like and want to stay in. Since there are millions of listings on the platform, you can utilize the filters to help narrow it down, so you're not scrolling for hours. Guests can view pictures, amenities, features, and descriptions of the various listings to better understand what they are getting into. There are also reviews left by previous guests. This helps each guest get a better idea of what the service is like and what other people's experiences have been. The higher the rating, the better the experience is likely to be.

Once the guest finds a listing that they like, they can go ahead and book it. There are additional prompts that they are taken through to pay and confirm the booking. In most cases, the booking request goes to the host to be confirmed, and then the payment process will continue. The exception to this is if the listing has an instant booking option. This allows them to skip the host verification step and book immediately.

Hosts

The process for a host is a bit more detailed because you have to create your listing and ensure everything is in order. There are plenty of options for Airbnb hosts, so regardless of the type of property you have, you will likely find an option that will suit you. You can rent out an entire property, just a room, a shared room, or a specific portion of the property. There is even an option to list events on the platform.

You will need to create an account with Airbnb. This account is completely free, but in some areas it may vary, so it is a good idea to look at the fees and restrictions that will affect you. Certain areas might also have restrictions on Airbnb or rental properties in general. It is wise to research if any of these apply to you and your property. To complete your account, you will follow the prompts and upload the necessary documents and files. You will also need to ensure that your listing looks attractive so people will want to book with you. This means you need to write a description, upload pictures, and create a title for your listing. You will also be able to set a price. The price is completely up to you, but it is a good idea to set a competitive price, as setting it too high won't get you that many bookings.

You will also be directed to a calendar function where you can indicate when your property will be available to rent out. Some people only rent out their property during certain months; others do it throughout the year. It is completely up to you, so you can decide what will work best for your schedule. Once you have completed your information and followed all the prompts, you can publish your listing. Then, all you have to do is wait for people to start booking with you. This is just the basic overview of how Airbnb works for a host, but we will dive into more in-depth steps throughout the book.

IS AIRBNB SAFE?

One of the biggest concerns that people have is whether Airbnbs are safe or not. The platform creators have developed many systems and tools to ensure the safety of both guests and hosts. Identity verification, reviewing procedures, and private internal messaging make it much safer for both parties. Since payment is made through the platform, money can be held until check-in. This provides security to the guest, as they know they will not lose their money. Many people are scared of being scammed, so the fact that the host is not paid until after check-in reassures the guests.

Multiple verification methods are put in place for both hosts and guests. Both will have to enter personal details that must be confirmed. As a host, you can see how much information somebody has uploaded. The more information somebody provides, the more trustworthy they are likely to be. The same goes for guests who are looking for trustworthy hosts. The review system is an incredibly valuable part of the platform. Both guests and hosts review each other. This means you will be able to see any negative reviews about a potential guest, and they would be able to see the same about you. This helps you to make better choices when you are accepting a booking request.

With all of this being said, there have been some Airbnb horror stories. Before this puts you off, consider the fact that Airbnb is a massive company. There are likely to be a few bad experiences with the millions of properties worldwide that advertise with Airbnb. Airbnb does its best to help mitigate the situation and ensure that any guest or host that does not meet the standards is permanently removed. Since Airbnb cannot be in direct contact with every guest and every host, it is best to ensure that you take precautions to ensure your safety. We will be diving more into the nitty-gritty of this in later chapters.

2

DIFFERENT TYPES OF AIRBNB ACCOMMODATIONS

One of the biggest draws of Airbnb is the fact that there are many different types of accommodations for a guest to choose from and that a host can list. This gives incredible flexibility to all parties. Understanding the types of accommodation you can list on the platform will allow you to make better investment decisions, especially if you are looking to purchase a new property to list on Airbnb.

FOUR MAIN TYPES OF PLACES OFFERED VIA AIRBNB

Airbnb offers extreme flexibility for a host. You can rent out any type of space as long as customers are looking for that particular type of rental. There are four main types of places that Airbnb offers. We're going to dive into these now.

- **Entire Place**: The traveler will book the whole property for themselves and will not have to share the space with anybody else. An entire property could include a garden, a pool, and other amenities.
- **Private Rooms**: This is a larger property divided into common areas for the guests. A guest will have their own bedroom and possibly bathroom, but share the other amenities with other guests.
- **Hotel Rooms**: These are simply hotel rooms that are rented out on Airbnb.
- **Shared Rooms**: This is similar to hostel-style living. It is targeted more toward younger travelers because it will be a room with multiple beds where the amenities are shared by everyone.

SPECIALIZED ACCOMMODATIONS

In addition to the four main types offered on Airbnb, there are many specialized accommodation types that you can list. This provides even more flexibility to both the host and the guests.

Airbnb for Work

This is a spinoff from Airbnb, which allows corporations to use the platform to make bookings for business trips. It allows a business to plan trips for their employees and to keep track of the bookings that have been made. The more 5-star reviews that your property gets from business travelers, the more likely it will show up on Airbnb's work trip feed. There are also a few other criteria that need to be met in order to show up on this filter. For example, you would need to have high-speed Wi-Fi, well-equipped workstations, after-hour access, be close to transportation and cities, and possibly offer on-site laundry facilities. All of this provides for the needs of a business person who is traveling into town for a meeting or other business purpose.

Airbnb Plus

Airbnb Plus is reserved for the finest quality homes with great reviews. In order to become an Airbnb Plus host, you will need to be verified by Airbnb. There will also be an in-person inspection to make sure that you fit the criteria. You will definitely need to put in some extra effort in order to gain this status. It comes with additional maintenance requirements as you will need to provide above and beyond what other Airbnb hosts generally offer. This might mean that you need to ensure that your kitchen is stocked with amenities like cooking oil, basic cooking supplies, dishes, and cutlery. You might also need to stock your bathrooms with hair care products, bubble bath, high-quality bathing products, and other amenities. Your property also needs to have something different about it. Exceptional design is part of the qualifications that are required.

Airbnb Luxe

This option allows travelers to access amazing properties as well as trip designers to help them plan their experience. These homes are hand-picked from around the world and pass a very strict verification process. Standards need to be met in both design and function, as well as 300 different criteria. This is not just about offering guests great accommodation, but ensuring their trip is transformational and unforgettable. It is essentially about creating an experience.

Unique Stays

Many travelers out there are looking for unique experiences and uncommon spaces to rent out. These are non-traditional properties or spaces that can be rented out on the platform. There are so many types of unique stays that are available, so if you have a property that fits the bill, you will be able to utilize it for Airbnb. Perhaps you have a houseboat, a yurt, or a treehouse. There are even igloos are available on the platform.

Properties Run by Superhosts

In order to achieve Superhost status, you need to complete 100 nights of hosting over three completed stays or have ten completed stays over a period of a year, maintain a 90 percent response rate, have less than a 1 percent cancellation rate, and maintain a rating of 4.8. There are many guests out there who adjust the filters to look for Superhosts. Since a Superhost needs to meet these additional criteria, the guests can be sure that they are in for a good experience. It is definitely worth your while to try and earn this status.

It does take a bit of work to get there, but if you can maintain quality standards you will be able to become a Superhost. There are many incentives that are offered when you are a Superhost. You will be able to charge a bit more in your pricing since you have been verified and meet the higher standards. You will also get dedicated Airbnb support, improvement in listing visibility, and a badge signifying your Superhost status.

The fact that there are so many options available on Airbnb means that you will likely find one that's going to work for you. You can offer specialized accommodation or simply fit into one of the four primary categories. Either way, you will be able to make some good money through Airbnb if you utilize the right strategies. In the next chapter, we are going to be looking at being an Airbnb host and what it is really like.

3

THE TRUTH ABOUT AIRBNB HOSTING—MYTH VS. REALITY

Many people are put off from using Airbnb because of the many myths that surround it. It is really helpful to be able to see what is true and what is a lie. This way, you will be able to move into your Airbnb journey with confidence.

MYTH 1: THE VACATION RENTAL INDUSTRY IS SKETCHY

There are so many people out there who think the vacation rental industry is sketchy. The truth is that vacation rentals have been organized by individual property owners for many, many years. The only difference between Airbnb and other privately owned vacation rentals is that the platform makes it a lot easier for people to connect with each other. Airbnb is simply a place for property owners and travelers to meet. Previously, it was a lot more difficult to find a private property owner who offered a unique place to stay. Now, it is just more convenient.

MYTH 2: BEING A HOST MEANS YOU CAN'T GO ANYWHERE ELSE

A common myth is that you will never be able to leave your property. If you are somebody who loves to travel and spend time away from your home, this belief may keep you from pursuing an Airbnb business opportunity. However, there are plenty of options available to you if you want to leave your property and travel. In most cases, you are not going to be expected to stay on-site while you have guests. Unless you are providing a service to them each day, you really don't need to be there to babysit. This is especially true if you have private property or private rooms that are being rented out. Most of the time, people want to be left alone, so if you have ensured that everything is up to date and maintained on your property, then you are not likely to need to be there at all.

With this being said, it is always a good idea to have somebody available who will be able to assist your guests if necessary. You could hire a property manager to handle all the affairs of your property while you travel and do the things you enjoy. Another option would be to have a friend or someone else that you know take care of the property while you go on holiday.

MYTH 3: AIRBNB IS ONLY PROFITABLE IN THE WEST

If you do not live in the west, a common myth is that your Airbnb is not going to be successful. This is definitely not true. Although Airbnb was started in San Francisco and founded by Americans, it has expanded to the rest of the world. There are over 7 million active listings across the world. These listings span 100,000 cities in 220 countries and territories.[1] There are millions of hosts worldwide, and they are making good money out of it. People want to be able to travel all over the world, not just in the west. Airbnb has a global approach to ensure that it thrives all over the world. You will be able to receive payment in your local currency and the platform allows you to process those payments easily.

MYTH 4: AIRBNB GUESTS ARE MOSTLY PARTY PEOPLE WHO CAUSE TROUBLE AND DESTROY FURNITURE

This myth is fueled by a few horror stories that have come to light. The truth is, there have been some bad experiences for hosts who have had to deal with crazy partygoers who have ruined their property. With 103.7 million stays in the second quarter of 2022 alone, if there are one or two bad experiences that come out of it, it really is not that much.[2] Not only that, but Airbnb does take these things very seriously and will ban guests from using the platform if there is a reason to do so.

Even if you do have a bad experience with a guest at your Airbnb, the chances that it will be a massive blow to your income and your property are quite small. When dealing with people, there's always going to be the possibility of having a bad guest experience. These things are quite easy to handle and typically blow over. If you take the time to screen your guests before you confirm the bookings, you shouldn't really have an issue finding decent houseguests. Communication is always important so that you can set the standard for what you expect from your guests. This will prevent potential miscommunications down the line.

MYTH 5: BECOMING AN AIRBNB HOST IS ONLY ABOUT BUSINESS

Some people truly want to run Airbnb as a business, and that is completely valid. However, there are other people who do not want to do that. Either way, how you want to run your Airbnb is going to be completely up to you. Becoming an Airbnb host is not solely about business. When it first started, it was about offering experiences and making connections. If this is your main motivation, then this is what you can offer to your guests. Of course, making a profit is a big part of running an Airbnb, but your true motivation could lie in the hospitality side of it.

Airbnb is different from traditional hotels and formal vacation rentals. You are allowed to make it feel as homey as you would like. It is an expression of your creativity and hospitality. People know that when they book with Airbnb, they are not going to get a crisp, clean, and formal experience. They'd rather get something that feels a bit more personal. If you are passionate about hospitality and want to open your doors to strangers so that you can form new connections and relationships, then let this be your motivation and run with it. That extra-special personal touch is what has gotten many people 5-star reviews.

MYTH 6: AIRBNB RENTALS ARE BAD FOR MY NEIGHBORHOOD

People love comfort and things that stay exactly the same. The problem with this is that comfort does not often lead to growth or improvement. If you look at anything good that has happened over the past few years, you will see that it came about due to some sort of change. Many people are quite afraid of inviting Airbnb rentals into their area because they think it's going to lead to neighborhood deterioration. This is definitely a myth, and the opposite is actually true. When you invite more tourists into your area, you are spurring on the economy. You're leading to more economic growth for small businesses and for the people who live in the neighborhood.

Adding new people to the area also introduces diversity and allows for new thoughts and ideas. You will find that neighborhoods that open themselves up to new cultures and experiences are ones that tend to grow. If a neighborhood has growth potential, then more money would be invested in it, and the quality of life would increase for those who live there.

Of course, this can be a scary process if you are somebody who is not used to change, but it is absolutely worth it because the positives definitely outweigh any potential negatives. Airbnb is simply an advancement of an already established industry. It is something that has always existed but has now been improved upon. In the next chapter, we will look at helping you decide whether starting your own Airbnb business is the right decision for you.

4

9 SIGNS STARTING AN AIRBNB BUSINESS IS RIGHT FOR YOU

To date, Airbnb hosts have earned more than $150 billion. With 14,000 new hosts joining every single month, that number is only going to increase.[1] While this is enticing, it is important to understand whether Airbnb is right for you. Here are a few things you should consider and ask yourself before moving forward.

SIGN #1: YOU HAVE A KNACK FOR HOSPITALITY

Hospitality is definitely a talent, and there are many people who have it. If you are somebody who genuinely enjoys hosting people and doesn't mind playing hotel manager, then this could be the perfect fit for you. You will be able to invite many different people from all over the world into your home. You can cater to them and ensure that they are having a good time while they staying with you.

SIGN #2: THE MARKET CONDITIONS ARE THERE

Above all, Airbnb is designed to help you make some money. If you're unable to make a profit, it is definitely not going to be worth your time and effort. This is why it is so important to understand the market conditions where you are. There should be enough demand in your area or in the area you are looking to purchase a new property. This demand should be sufficient to facilitate your business and make financial sense.

You should have a look at whether your property is somewhere that people want to stay. This is why it is so important to do research about your area. It doesn't make sense to start an Airbnb and put all your time and effort into it if nobody wants to book in your neighborhood. Areas that have a high demand for tourism or business travelers tend to do better with Airbnb because there is a constant stream of people booking with you. Have a look to see how many other Airbnbs are in your area or how many other rental properties there are in general. Then see if they have a high occupancy rate. This just means how often the properties are booked out. That will give you a good idea about the viability of an Airbnb business in your current area.

SIGN #3: YOU'RE IN IT FOR MORE THAN JUST A QUICK BUCK

Building an Airbnb business takes some time. You are not going to be raking it in from the first moment you click publish on your listing. As with any business, it does take some patience in order to develop a successful long-term business. If you are not somebody who is able to put the necessary time and effort into your Airbnb business, this might not be the right option for you.

SIGN #4: YOU HAVE ENOUGH STARTING CAPITAL

An Airbnb business is not something that you can start up with absolutely nothing in your bank account. You need to have some start-up capital in order to get your property ready or purchase a new one. If you are looking to purchase a new property to start your Airbnb business, then you will need a good amount of start-up capital. Even if you are going to be hosting a property that you already own, you still need money to get your property Airbnb-ready.

Airbnb is not just about simply renting out an extra room in your house. You need to be able to create an experience for your guests. This means that you need to purchase new linen, furniture, and decor. You are trying to create a good experience for your guests, so you can't just use anything that you find in your house. You will need to purchase plenty of new things in order to get those good reviews from your guests. If you simply throw in the old lounge set from your 20s and the bed that you no longer use because it is now uncomfortable, you are not going to be able to run a successful business. Start-up costs are just part of the deal when it comes to running any successful business.

SIGN #5: IT'S ACTUALLY ALLOWED IN YOUR JURISDICTION

Not every area is going to be welcoming to Airbnb. There are various legalities, rules, and restrictions that might come into play depending on your area. You need to ensure that your Airbnb business will be legal. Make sure to check locally to ensure that you are allowed to run an Airbnb out of your property. You should also ensure that you understand the restrictions that apply if you are allowed to rent out your property as an Airbnb. This is definitely one of the biggest things that you should consider when getting into Airbnb. You might need to purchase a property outside of your current location in order to start up your business.

SIGN #6: YOU HAVE ENOUGH TIME AND ENERGY

It is definitely possible to start up your Airbnb as a side hustle, but you do need to have time to put into it. This is especially so when you are trying to get things off the ground. You'll need to make sure that your property is good to go, and this does take some time and effort. Once your property has been listed on Airbnb and is ready to receive guests, you need to have time to tend to your guests' demands and turn over the property for new guests. Maintenance and cleaning are all part of the deal when it comes to running an Airbnb, so you need to take this into consideration.

SIGN #7: YOU'RE OK WITH THE COSTS

It is so important that you are realistic about the costs involved with running an Airbnb. There are definitely one-time costs that need to be considered. However, the costs don't just stop once you have listed your home on Airbnb. There are recurring costs that need to be taken into consideration when you are running your business. For example, you would need to provide your guests with certain things in order to help them enjoy their stay. Perhaps you are providing them with a welcome basket, shampoo, body wash, basic cooking essentials, basic cleaning essentials, and similar items. All of these things will need to be replaced once they have been used.

You might also need to think about bringing in a cleaning or maintenance service to help you out. This is also going to incur costs. This is why it is important for you to sit down and make a budget for yourself so that you understand exactly how much money it is going to cost you to run an Airbnb business. This will help you prepare for the future and make sure that you have a realistic idea of how much profit you will be making.

SIGN #8: YOU HAVE ENOUGH RISK TOLERANCE

Like with any business, there are some risks to take into account when you are investing in an Airbnb business. There are financial and personal risks that come with this kind of endeavor. You need to be completely honest with yourself and sit down to discover what level of risk you are comfortable with and if this is the right option for you.

SIGN #9: YOU ARE COMFORTABLE WITH STRANGERS IN YOUR HOME

There are some people who are quite touchy about letting strangers into their personal and private spaces. This doesn't mean that you are not a hospitable person. It just means that you are uncomfortable with people invading your space. If this is the case, then Airbnb is probably not going to be the best option for you. Think about whether you are open to the idea of people you don't know using your facilities and sleeping under the same roof as you. It is completely understandable if this is not something that appeals to you. However, it is important that you be honest with yourself so that you don't start something that you, later on, find out that you just don't enjoy.

The truth is, being an Airbnb host is not for everyone. However, if you are willing to take the risk and if you have what it takes, the payoff can be huge. Running an Airbnb does have a monetary benefit, but the benefits extend far beyond this. You will be able to expand your knowledge and broaden your horizons based on the people that you invite to your home. It is truly an enjoyable experience if this is something you know you are well fit for. In the next chapter, we are going to cover the Airbnb framework that you can use to jumpstart your own Airbnb business.

5

THE "AIRBNB FRAMEWORK" FOR STARTING YOUR OWN SUCCESSFUL AIRBNB BUSINESS

You don't have to be a genius or a visionary or even a college graduate to be successful. You just need a framework and a dream.

— MICHAEL DELL

THE "AIRBNB FRAMEWORK"

The rest of this book is going to be organized into six separate parts. These parts are going to go through the framework for creating a successful Airbnb business. There will be a lot to cover in each of these sections, and when you put everything together, you will be able to run a very successful Airbnb business. In this chapter, we are just going to give a summary of what this framework is like for creating a prosperous Airbnb business.

Analyze (Chapters 6–8)

The first stage of this process is going to be analysis. Whenever you start a business, you need to have all the facts before you get going. This helps you to understand the environment and what your goals are. You will also need to look at the competition so that you can assess the viability of your business plan. Proper analysis is fundamental to any effective plan.

Insurance (Chapters 9–10)

When it comes to renting out a property, insurance is so important. If you do not have insurance, then you're putting yourself at risk of losing money and other valuable items. This is why we have to spend some time talking about insurance in general and what insurance you need to have.

Ready Your Property (Chapters 11–15)

The third step is all about getting ready for your guests. At the end of the day, an Airbnb business is all about the property and making your guests happy. If you are able to do this, you will encourage good reviews and get continuous business. This is an incredibly important part of the process and something that needs to be concentrated on. Another thing to note is that preparing your property is going to be a constant thing. You will always need to ensure that it is at its best at all times. This will make sure that every guest who steps through your doors has a great experience.

Booking Management (Chapters 16–19)

Being able to manage your bookings is an integral part of running an Airbnb business. You need to ensure that the process is easy to follow and efficient. This will remove a lot of stress from you and your guests and make it a lot easier to manage who stays in your Airbnb and all the details surrounding that process.

Get Noticed (Chapters 20–25)

Getting noticed is really important if you want to bring in as many new guests as possible. If your listing is not eye-catching and doesn't draw the attention of people scrolling through the platform, you will not be able to make a lot of money through Airbnb investing. This is why it is so important to do what you can to get yourself noticed. There are many strategies and tips that you can put into place, and in this section, you will be able to learn everything you need to.

Build Relationships (Chapters 26–27)

It is really important to develop good relationships with your guests. This will result in them wanting to come back and stay with you. If you have many returning guests, you will know that they will be taking care of your property, and you can trust them with your space. It also allows you to have more security in terms of bookings. You know that a few good people will be booking your property every once in a while. This is incredibly important to building a good business.

There are definitely many different paths that you can take when you are starting your own Airbnb business. The Airbnb framework is a very simple six-step process that will help you to start any Airbnb business from the ground up. It doesn't matter how much experience you have in hospitality or even building a business. In the next chapter, we are going to go over the first step of the process—analyzing the market.

STAGE 1

ANALYZING THE MARKET

6

HOW TO ANALYZE THE PLAYING FIELD

In the US alone, there are over 660,000 Airbnb listings.[1] There are a ton of people who are making their dreams come true through real estate investing. There are different ways to identify who your competitors are and their place in the market. Not all of those 660,000 listings are successful. The ones that will be successful are the ones that put themselves in the most profitable position. This starts with being able to analyze what you are working with. Then you are able to make the right decisions for the current market.

TOOLS YOU'LL NEED

There are many different tools that you can utilize in order to help you with your analysis. These are easy to use and quite easy to access as well. Some of them might require you to pay some sort of fee in order to use them, but most of them are free.

AirDNA

The first tool we are going to be talking about is AirDNA. This platform provides research and analytics software. It helps you to understand how the short-term rental industry is changing over time. You will be able to dig deeper into the rental market using this tool. You can get trend reports and forecasts to help you make your decisions and understand exactly what is going on in your market. As a host, you will have access to granular insights that are behind the industry and the business.

AllTheRooms

This is a great tool that provides business insights and analytics. This is specific to the vacation rental industry. It includes multiple key features such as market intelligence, property intelligence, and competitive intelligence. This will help you to get a more in-depth look at what is happening in your area so that you are able to make better decisions regarding your rental property.

Facebook Hosting Groups

There are multiple Facebook hosting groups on the platform. You can join them and gain insight into what is going on in your market. It helps to connect with other Airbnb hosts so you can see what they're doing and what their strategies are. In most cases, other hosts are quite happy to share their knowledge and insights with people that are new to the market. If you can find a great community of people who are willing to give you one-on-one advice, this is going to be incredibly valuable to you. You can ask specific questions and get advice on what you are currently struggling with. It also helps just to have other people around you who are going through the same process. You will feel supported and most likely be able to develop better strategies for your Airbnb.

I have created a Facebook group for hosts to share, learn, get advice, and find support from other people who are going through the same thing. Everyone is welcome to join, so you can extend the invite to other Airbnb hosts you might know. This is a private group, so you can feel free to share, knowing that only the people who are going through the host journey will be able to see and respond. Please feel free to join. I would love to have you!

Here are the details:

Name: Airbnb Host Community

URL: www.facebook.com/groups/airbnbhostcommunity

QR Code:

FACTORS TO CONSIDER

When you are doing your analysis, before you start investing in Airbnb, you need to look at a few key factors. These factors will allow you to get a holistic view of how profitable your Airbnb will be. You will also be able to develop strategies that are specific to you, and that will let you know what will work for your area and your property.

Destination

When it comes to investing in property, location is key. Even if you already have a property that you want to turn into an Airbnb, you still need to understand the ins and outs of the location and if it's going to work for short-term rentals. If you think about it, people would rather stay in an average Airbnb that is located centrally to what they want to do and see than stay in an amazing property that does not allow them to see the sights they want to see or be surrounded by the environment they want to be in. This is why it is so important to think about the location. You can pretty much change anything about your property except for the location, so don't skip this step.

People often book holidays based on location and not on the accommodation that they're going to stay in. Once they decide on the location, they will then start looking for rentals in that area. This is not to say that the other aspects of your Airbnb are not important. It is just simply to note that location is typically the first thing that people consider, which is the reason why it is so important.

When you are looking at your current location or the location you want to invest in, you need to understand a few things. The first thing you should think about is seasonality. This means knowing when the high and low seasons are. When are people flocking to this area and when are people staying away? This will help you to understand the times of the year which will be the most profitable and why people are coming to the area at this time. It also allows you to price your properties appropriately at various seasons so that you can ensure you are making a good profit. Things like major holidays and events also impact how many people are coming to an area. If you live in an area that has big festivals or events, you know the people who want to stay at rental properties during this time.

Beyond simply understanding the important dates that guests are going to be coming to your area, you also need to understand what the place has to offer. Restaurants, sightseeing spots, landmarks, parks, and activities are all really important to the location. Guests will often look for local attractions and suggestions for things that they could be doing while they're in your city or your area. The better the facilities that surround your Airbnb, the more popular it will be. If your guest simply wants to relax and enjoy the time, it is reassuring to know that there are plenty of restaurants, stores, and activities around the property. This will result in a much better retention rate.

Target Market

The next thing to consider is your target market. This typically goes hand-in-hand with the location, as there will be a specific type of person that wants to visit a specific type of place. Not only that, certain people will gravitate toward certain types of properties as well. If you understand who your target audience is, then you will be able to tailor your property to meet their needs. You should be realistic about who this target market is as there are going to be some limitations based on your property.

Certain types of people will be more attracted to certain cities, areas, and properties. Your city's tourism website as well as active Airbnb listings will give you a good idea of the demographics. Think about whether your city attracts more leisure tourists or business people. If tourists frequent the area, you can think about whether these tourists are coming in groups, families, singles, or couples. Think about what kind of amenities they are looking for and what they are willing to pay for these amenities. All of this information will help you tailor your property to what your target guests need. This will help you with marketing as well as the general provisions of your property. You will also be able to understand what kind of people are going to be staying with you.

Local Regulations

Many cities and states have decided to regulate rental properties and alternative lodging in different areas. This means that every property investor needs to understand the regulations in the area they want to invest in. You don't want to be put in a situation where you get in trouble with your local government for not sticking to the rules. You also don't want to put all this money into your Airbnb, only to realize that you have to shut it down a few years or months later. It is a good idea to consult your municipality and HOA to get all the information that you need about your property and what you are allowed to do. Once you have this information, you might have peace of mind in your area, or you might need to look into investing in another city or state.

Competitors

Understanding your competitors in the area is really important. You can do this by finding a few similar properties and using them as a benchmark for yours. Make sure that the properties you look at are ones that are offering the same type of service that you are. It's not really going to make sense to compare yourself to a five-bedroom, self-catering house when you have a two-bedroom guest house. Look for properties that are going to be your closest competitors and go from there.

You will need to look for competitors in the same or nearby neighborhoods. The properties need to have a similar configuration to yours. This just means having the same number of bedrooms, bathrooms, and comparable amenities. Once you have found a few properties that are similar to yours, you need to do some investigation. Have a look at how many competitors there are in your area. If there are too many, you might struggle to get guests. If there are too few, it might be a good idea to find out why there aren't as many Airbnbs in that area. You can also have a look at the pricing and how much of the calendar is open. The pricing will give you a good idea of what people are charging. If you look at the calendar, you will be able to see how in demand the area and the type of property are. You can cross-examine the pricing and the calendars. This way, you can get a good idea of what pricing gets the most bookings.

It is also a good idea to have a look at the reviews that are on the properties. Try and find out why the reviews were good or bad. This way you will be able to avoid bad ratings and provide your guests with the things that they were missing in the other properties. Once you have evaluated your competition, you can have a look at your own strategy and see what you need to change. You might notice that your pricing is not optimal for the market, and you can tweak this a little. Perhaps you could look into providing a few more amenities for your guests to enjoy on your property. Simply having a look at your competitors and what they are offering is a really good way to help improve your Airbnb strategy.

Financial Considerations

When you're investing, it means that you have to put some money in order to get money out. Your investment needs to make sense for you, and you need to be sure that you will be getting a good return on your investment. It is definitely a good idea to take the financials into consideration before you start investing or start putting your plan into practice. You can calculate your potential rental income, but you also need to understand the expenses that come with running your own Airbnb. All the money you make from your daily rates is not going to be just for profit. You will need to use some of that money to keep your property running smoothly and for other business costs.

Your financial considerations are not just going to be limited to purchasing a new property or renovating the one you currently have. There are going to be some continuous costs that you will need to take into consideration. These are going to be your expenses. Any money you make through your rental needs to be able to cover your expenses and then have a bit left over for your project. Here are a few things that you should be considering in terms of expenses you might incur while running an Airbnb:

- Inspection fees
- Repairs
- Furniture
- Insurance
- Utilities
- Maintenance
- Property tax
- Rental income tax
- Cleaning fees
- Hosting fees

This is definitely not everything that you need to consider when it comes to your expenses. However, it gives you a good idea of what to expect.

When it comes to performing market analysis for your Airbnb, there are many things that you need to consider. The above factors will help you develop a plan and a strategy to better understand the market. You will find that making decisions is a lot easier when you have all the information in front of you. It might seem like a long and tedious task, but it is definitely worth it. In the next chapter, we are going to compare the different types of properties that you can rent out.

7

PROS AND CONS OF RENTING OUT DIFFERENT PROPERTY TYPES

Airbnb recently announced 56 new vacation rental categories for over 4.4 million of its listings.[1] This means that now, more than ever, it is important for first-time Airbnb hosts to think about their property and how they can make it stand out. Not only that, but it opens up the door of opportunity for you to rent out whatever kind of space you have. Some of the categories that have been opened up are camping, design, and amazing pools. If you have a property with a unique feature or that is in a unique area, you can definitely use this to your advantage and get noticed more.

Different types of properties will need different strategies to help them stand out. It is important to consider what type of property you have to purchase when you are getting into short-term real estate investing. In this chapter, we are going to take a look at the many different types of rental properties that are available. It will give you a good idea of the unique strengths and weaknesses of the various property types. This will allow you to make better decisions and create a better strategy for yourself going forward.

DIFFERENT TYPES OF RENTAL PROPERTIES

You might recall from Chapter 2 that there are four primary types of Airbnb accommodation. Along with this, there are more exotic types of accommodation available. With this being said, you will likely find similarities between unique stays and the four primary types of rentals that we are going to be talking about in this chapter.

Entire Place

The first option is to rent out the entire property. When doing this, your guest will have complete access to everything that is on the property. This might include the yard, pool, and all the other areas of the house. Renting out an entire property does not necessarily mean that it needs to be a house. You could also rent out an entire apartment, condo, or villa. However, there are some criteria that need to be met when renting out this type of property. Typically, a guest would be expecting a bedroom, cooking space, and a bathroom.

This is a great option for many guests because it allows them to have the amenities they need. If they are traveling in bigger groups or as a family, it is cheaper to book out an entire place and then prepare meals for themselves. It is also a good idea to book something like this if they are staying for a longer period of time. It can get pretty expensive to eat out or order in every single day. Providing a cooking space allows your guests to cater for themselves, and this brings down the cost of the overall holiday. Not only that, but your guests will be able to enjoy the privacy of having a property to themselves.

One thing to note is that this kind of property will be more expensive than others. You might be limiting your potential guests as single people or couples might not see the need to rent out an entire property. People who are looking to travel around and sightsee might also not want to book out this type of property as they will not be making full use of the amenities.

Private Rooms

A private room still offers privacy but on a budget. A private room will have a bedroom and usually a bathroom that is completely private. Other amenities, such as the living space or kitchen, will be shared with the other guests who stay on the property. If you have a spare room in your house that you are looking to rent out, offering a private room could be a good option. This way, you'll be able to make money from the spare space that you have and create privacy for yourself and your guests. If you are doing this, it might be a good idea to look into creating a separate entrance for your guests so they can come and go as they please, and it's not going to interrupt you and your life.

A private room is a great option for many guests. This is especially so when it is a single person or a couple who is looking to travel. They do not want to stay in their accommodation for long periods as they're looking to be out and about. They are also not too concerned with being able to cook and cater for themselves. Cooking might be an option if there is a communal kitchen available, but this is not necessary for many private room options.

Hotel Rooms

A hotel room offers a level of service that can be likened to traditional hotels. You might find these types of rooms available at lifestyle hotels, boutiques, bed-and-breakfasts, or similar properties. You will be able to charge a bit more for these types of accommodation since you will be offering a service that many other Airbnbs don't. Things like turndown service, breakfast, and cleaning would be expected. It is a great option if you have access to the property that would allow this and you have the funds to provide this or the time to do it yourself.

Shared Rooms

There are many guests who do not mind sharing space with other guests. These tend to be students and travelers who are on a budget. Essentially, you will be able to rent out your space, and the space will be shared amongst many different people. You can think of it more like a hostel or dorm-style room. There might be multiple beds and bunk beds in one room that people sleep in. All amenities on the property will be shared amongst the people who have booked with you.

It is important to note that many travelers might not want to use this option. Families and people who are older generally do not enjoy sharing rooms. However, you are opening up your side of the world to people who want to travel on a budget. This is a great option if you live in a more expensive part of the world that is known for its travel. People want to come to these areas and see them, but they might be on a budget. You'll be offering a place for them to sleep and store their belongings while they go out and see the sights and enjoy the activities.

The pricing for these types of rooms is much less than most other Airbnb options. However, since you will be having a lot more people booking with you since you have more space available, this will offset the cheaper nightly rate. It is likely that the people who book with you would not be staying for long periods of time as they will want to move on to the next destination. This means that the turnover time can be quite quick, and you would need to be ready to clean up and get the rooms ready for the next guest.

Each of the four different types of Airbnb accommodation has its own unique pros and cons when it comes to renting them out. Part of what should drive your decision on which type of listing to launch is also what's in your best financial interest. In the next chapter, we'll compare the profitability of different types of Airbnb listings.

8

WHAT'S THE MOST PROFITABLE TYPE OF AIRBNB LISTING?

On average, Airbnb guests tend to stay 2.4 times longer in Airbnbs than they do in hotels. This could be attributed to the fact that guests are looking for an experience rather than just a place to sleep at night. If you are able to create a really great place for your guests to stay, you will definitely attract them for a longer period of time and make more money. That being said, there are definitely some properties that are more profitable than others. Understanding which ones can help you make better decisions going forward.

CALCULATING PROFITABILITY

You need to be able to calculate your profitability for your future Airbnb. This will help you to understand how much money you can make with your property.

Key Variables

There are a few key variables that you should take into consideration when you're looking at how profitable your Airbnb could potentially be. Just remember that this is just going to be an estimation. Things might change over the years, so it is a good idea to regularly look at these variables and adjust your expectations accordingly.

Upfront Costs and Operating Expenditures

The first thing you're going to want to look at is the upfront costs and operating expenditures. These are the things that you will continuously be paying for throughout the life of your Airbnb business. This is the general cost of taking care of your property and ensuring that it is at its best. If you already live in the area, you should have a good idea of the maintenance and upkeep costs since you already own a property there. You can use it as a base point and then see if there are any additional costs that you need to include.

You also need to take into account things like taxes, insurance premiums, and platform fees. Your taxes will include property tax and the tax that you make from the profit of your business, so make sure you take both of these into consideration. We will be delving more into insurance in later chapters, but for now, you can just think of this as part of your operating expenditures. The next thing to look at is your platform fees. Every time you get a booking, you will be paying a fee for the platform to process the transaction. This could differ from area to area, so it is important to understand what applies to you.

Occupancy Rates

Your occupancy rate is going to be how often your property is booked out. It is almost impossible to have a 100 percent occupancy rate, so don't feel discouraged if you find that the percentage is lower than what you thought. You are in a good spot if you have around a 50 percent occupancy rate. You can work on increasing this as you see fit. It is pretty easy to work out an occupancy rate; all you need to do is take the days that your property has been booked out and divide that by the number of days it was available to be booked out. You can take this number and multiply it by 100 to get the occupancy rate as a percentage.

So, if your property was booked out for 62 days of the year and there were 120 days available for it to be booked out, your occupancy rate would be 51.7 percent.

62/120 x 100 = 51.7%

When working out your occupancy rate, it is important to take into consideration seasonal fluctuations. There will be times when people are just not going to be traveling as much and other ones where you are going to get an influx of people booking with you. Half of the year, your occupancy rate could be over 70 percent, and the next half could be 30 percent. This is something that you will need to gauge so that you get a good idea of your overall occupancy rate and how much you'll make on an annual basis.

Neighborhood Factors

There are multiple neighborhood factors that can increase or decrease the amount of money that you make through your property. Since Airbnb is a short-term rental service, you need to make sure that whatever area you are going to invest in is going to be best for short-term rentals. Long-term rentals are a completely different thing because people are looking for something different. When people are renting for the long term, they're looking for a place to settle down and be in a good neighborhood. However, this is not the same criteria as for short-term rentals. Short-term rentals are better in areas that provide experiences for the guests or conveniently meet their needs.

There are many tools you can use to help you do a neighborhood analysis. Here are a few that you can consider using:

- AirDNA
- Beyond Pricing
- Host Tools
- Price Labs
- Rate Genie
- Wheelhouse

EXPENSES BY ACCOMMODATION TYPE

Different property types will cost you more or less, depending. You'll need to work out your costs so that you can work out your profit based on the type of property you're looking to invest in. There are definitely pros and cons to the various types of properties you can choose from. It is all up to you, and you need to decide what is going to work best for you. Some of the costs we are going to be speaking about are going to stay the same regardless of the type of property, but most of them will change. You also have to take into consideration your area and other aspects that might impact the price of the listed expenses.

Business License

Certain jurisdictions and areas will require licenses, and you will also pay special taxes in order to run an Airbnb. The cost of these things will vary depending on your state and country. You can have a look at your local laws and regulations to make sure that you understand what you need to pay for and so that you don't incur any unexpected fees down the line.

Property Taxes

These are pretty much unavoidable regardless of where you live. Often, they are included in your mortgage payment, so it is easy to make the required installments. If it is not included in your mortgage, then you will need to make a big once-a-year payment. It is a good idea to save a little bit each month and then pay off your property taxes by the required date. This will make it a lot easier for you to pay, and it won't seem like you are just forking out a whole bunch of money once a year.

Housekeeping and Maintenance

If you are not going to take care of the cleaning and housekeeping yourself, then you'll need to pay somebody to do it. It is usually easier to have somebody come in and clean for you because you will free up time for yourself to work on other aspects of your business or continue working at your regular job. Housekeeping and maintenance are incredibly important because they allow you to get good reviews. Many people overlook how important a clean and well-maintained property is. If you do choose to clean it yourself, you will still need to cover the costs. Include the amount of money you will be spending on cleaning supplies in your expense list.

In terms of maintenance, you will need to put away some money just in case something happens that you need to take care of. If you own your own property, you already know that certain things always pop up. It might be an issue with the plumbing, or the home is in need of a fresh coat of paint. Regardless of what it is, sometimes these matters aren't visible until they actually need to be tended to. This is why it is a good idea to put aside a certain amount of money each month for maintenance costs. When something does happen that needs your attention, you will have the money to deal with it.

Insurance

Insurance is a really important part of running an Airbnb. There are always risks involved, so you need to be sure that you have good insurance and that all the important things are going to be covered.

Goods and Supplies

Typically, you are going to need to provide your guests with a few simple goods and supplies. When your guests live in your home, they are going to use these things. For example, toilet paper, soap, shampoo, coffee, tea, trash bags, and quite a few other disposable things. It would be a good idea for you to buy these things in bulk so that you lower the price of them, and you will always have them on hand so when you are turning over the property for the next guest, you can quickly replace what is needed.

Utilities

Water, gas, trash, sewage, electricity, and Wi-Fi are all important to any kind of rental property. All of those can be quite a big chunk of your expenses, so make sure that you have prepared for them. You don't really have a choice but to pay for these items, and there really isn't much you can do about it, so make sure you have the money available.

Airbnb Fees

Airbnb charges around 3 percent commission on all bookings. Sometimes this can differ based on area, so it is a good idea to check and see. However, you should expect a certain fee to be charged in addition to your booking fee. If you take this into consideration, then you will be able to charge a rate that will offset the fee so that you're not losing too much money.

There are many factors that you need to consider in order to find the most profitable way to rent out your property. You need to think about things like location, the type of property you have, the type of guest that is going to stay at your property, and a number of other things. Taking the time to understand your property and what you will be paying for is a really good way to estimate how much money you will be making from your Airbnb. In the next chapter, we are going to be diving into getting the right insurance for your Airbnb business.

STAGE 2

AIRBNB INSURANCE

9

AIRBNB INSURANCE—WHICH TYPE OF POLICY SHOULD YOU GET?

If you are just signing up for Airbnb, you might've heard that you can get automatic protection when you activate a listing. Many people believe that because of this, they do not need to get their own insurance. This is not necessarily true. This is why it's important to understand what kind of protection is included in Airbnb's insurance policy.

AIRBNB INSURANCE: WHAT EVERY HOST NEEDS TO KNOW

What exactly is covered by Airbnb AirCover? The main goal of this type of insurance cover is to protect the hosts from damage caused by guests. AirCover is completely free for every Airbnb host who signs up on the platform. Some of the things that are included in this insurance coverage are as follows:

- $1 million in liability insurance
- $3 million in damage protection
- Auto & boat
- Art & valuables
- Pet damage protection
- Deep cleaning protection
- Income loss protection

This may sound amazing, and you might feel pretty secure with this type of offering. However, this does not thoroughly protect your property. It definitely does reduce any out-of-pocket expenses for things like cleaning and damage, but the truth is that it is simply not comprehensive enough to replace regular insurance. In fact, it is not insurance at all. It is simply an alternative to insurance and was created as an incentive to use the platform.

The topic of insurance can be a complicated one, but it is something that you will need to be well versed in if you are going to be in the property business. There are multiple different types of insurance out there, and you need to know which one you should be getting. We are going to go through a few of the different types of insurance out there, and then you can decide which one is going to be the best one for you.

Homeowner's Insurance

Let's first start with homeowner's insurance. If you own a property, then it's very likely that you have this type of insurance. A homeowner's insurance policy will cover damages that are caused by natural disasters and other unforeseen circumstances. Things like fire, lightning, and hail are covered under homeowner's insurance. These things are not covered by Airbnb AirCover, so you can already see the difference here. The issue with homeowner's insurance is that it does not include any kind of business activity. Since most Airbnb hosts do not live at their rental properties, this will apply. If you do live on the property that you are renting out as an Airbnb, then there might be an exception to this, but it is important to check.

If you have homeowner's insurance and are renting out property that you do not stay at, it could be pretty risky. If your insurance company finds out that your home is not used by you and there is some damage that occurs, they will almost always reject your claim. This means that you will have to pay out-of-pocket for all of the damage that has taken place. If you are not living on the property, then homeowner's insurance is simply not going to be enough to cover your property.

Landlord Insurance

The next type of insurance that you can consider is landlord insurance. This includes casualty insurance and property insurance. This protects you, your tenants, and any other employees of the business. The biggest difference between homeowner's and landlord insurance is that the landlord insurance will offer income protection. What this means is that if your home is not fit for renters due to an unforeseen circumstance, like a natural disaster, your insurance policy will pay you your rental income. Landlord insurance does not cover things that are personal to your property, such as furniture, art, and appliances.

You will need to have a conversation with your insurance provider because many landlord insurance policies don't actually cover short-term rentals. If you are planning on renting out your Airbnb for more than a month, then landlord insurance could be a good option for you, but if it's less than 30 days, it's not going to be of many benefits. However, you can consider something like home-sharing insurance if you are just renting out one of your rooms on the property while you are still living in the main house.

Commercial Property Insurance

Commercial, home-sharing, or vacation rental policies are good options if you are choosing to rent out your property as a true Airbnb with consecutive short-term guests. A commercial property policy is also known as a business property policy. This is definitely one of the most common options. If you do not live on your property and are only using it for short-term rentals, it is possibly your best option. This type of insurance will cover liability and property. This means that damage to your property or any damage or injuries that happen to your guests will all be covered.

Umbrella Policies

An umbrella policy is simply an extension of liability coverage that is typically offered in homeowner's or landlord policies. These will reimburse you for any damages incurred above what has been outlined in the underlying policy. For example, if one of your guests gets injured due to a fault on the property and then decides to sue you, your homeowner's or landlord insurance will pay the initial claim. Anything over and above that will be covered by the umbrella policy. A blanket umbrella possibly covers properties in multiple cities or states. This makes it a really good option for any Airbnb investor who has properties in more than one place. You should make sure that you understand what will be covered by your umbrella policy and how it will all work. Not all of them will work exactly the same, so doing research is of the utmost importance.

There are definitely many things to consider when you are choosing an insurance policy for your Airbnb business. Although you will automatically get AirCover, it only provides certain types of protection for the host. This is simply not enough and should be supplemented with additional insurance coverage. In the next chapter, we will discuss some practical safety tips you can apply as an Airbnb host to help minimize any damage incurred.

10

SAFETY TIPS FOR HOSTS

While you might've heard that it can be dangerous for guests, the truth is that less than 0.1 percent of all stays result in serious safety issues.[1] This is quite a small statistic, so is it something to worry about? The truth is, it is the host's responsibility to make sure that nothing bad happens to the guest. Even though there is a very small chance that anything will happen, it is good to be prepared and make sure that you put in place the best safety practices that you can.

MOST COMMON PROBLEMS THAT HOSTS FACE

There can definitely be some unexpected situations that pop up when you are a host. However, you can prepare for the most common ones so that you're not completely caught off guard if they do happen.

Payment Disputes

Payment disputes tend to be quite common when you are renting out your property to short-term visitors. However, when you're using the Airbnb platform, these are not things that you would typically have to worry about. Since all payments are handled through the platform, it is a lot safer than dealing one-on-one with the customer. Both the guest and the host are protected in terms of payments.

Physical Injuries to Guests

If a guest gets injured on your property due to negligence or there is an issue with a facility that is on your property, they can sue you. This is why it is so important to have insurance to cover this and to make sure that your property is safe. Doing an inspection of your property every few months will help minimize the risk of this happening.

Theft of Personal Belongings or High-Valued Possessions

As much as you would like to believe that everybody who stays on your property is going to take care of your possessions and not steal them, this is definitely something that can happen. It's a risk you take when you are an Airbnb host. This is why it's best to not leave any kind of high-value possessions or personal belongings at the rental property. Do your best to ensure that anything that you deem valuable is not going to be there. This way, you can have peace of mind when your guests stay with you. Insurance usually covers theft and loss of belongings, but make sure that your insurance policy does include this.

Property Damage

Property damage is also a common risk that you have to think about. If you have a good insurance policy, then this will be covered. It is important to screen your guests as best as possible to make sure that they are responsible. With this being said, there really is only so much that you find out about your guests. There will always be a risk of property damage when other people are using your facilities.

BEST SAFETY PRACTICES FOR AIRBNB HOSTS

Even though there are plenty of risks that come with renting out your property to strangers, there are things that you can do to keep yourself and your property safe. If you stick to these safety practices, then you will significantly minimize the risk of having to deal with any unfortunate situations.

Only Interact Using Airbnb's Platform

It might seem beneficial to take all your business dealings off the platform because you would be able to skip the Airbnb fee and do things the way you want to. However, this is typically not the best idea because it can leave you vulnerable to certain situations. The platform has been designed in such a way as to protect both the guest and the host. When a guest puts in a request to book certain dates, you have the opportunity to look at their profile and find out more about them. If you take things off the platform, you do not have access to profiles, reviews, or references. Everything is simply left to chance.

Be Clear with House Rules, House Manual, and Expectations

The Airbnb platform will allow a host to create a house manual and rules and then upload them. This is completely visible to the guests, so they know what is going to be expected of them if they stay with you. This allows you to hold your guests accountable to the expectations that you set. You know that they have access to the rules and manual, so there really isn't an excuse for them to misuse any of your items. You can put in any type of rule that you deem fit. Your rules can include things like smoking, quiet hours, wearing shoes in the house, or Wi-Fi usage.

Even though setting these rules is really important, you have to be mindful of not overdoing them. If you set unnecessary rules, then people are going to be turned off from booking with you. At the end of the day, people still want to enjoy their holiday, and they don't want to be thinking about whether or not they can do certain things at home. You still want to make them feel comfortable and welcome in your home, but set a few guidelines so that it protects you both.

Have the Right Insurance

As you already know, insurance is of the utmost importance. Make sure that you do thorough research and get the right insurance for you. It is also a good idea to shop around for insurance. You don't want to pay more than you actually need to because insurance can be a costly expense. If you compare quotes from various insurers, then you can be sure that you are getting the best deal and the best coverage.

Get a Security Deposit for Every Stay

It is definitely in your best interest to ask for a security deposit from your guests. In the event of some minor damage, you will be able to dip into the security deposit and pay for it. Some damages don't really warrant an insurance claim, so collecting a security deposit means that you are not going to be expected to foot the bill for damages that were caused by the carelessness of the guest. If there was no damage, then the guest gets the security deposit back. Doing this actually helps keep the guest accountable because they want to get their money back, so they aren't going to be as careless.

Have a Security System Installed

A security system is a great investment for both your protection and that of your guests. You will be able to protect your home even when you are not there. It also helps you to keep tabs on everything that is going on. You will be able to automate things like the thermostat, locking up the doors, and the lights. One thing to note is that you will not be able to install security cameras in certain places that would be considered to be an invasion of your guests' privacy. If there are cameras on the outside of the property, then make sure you have notified your guests about this and understand the laws that surround things like this.

Add Smoke and Carbon Monoxide Detectors

Adding these two things helps give your guests peace of mind, and it also protects your property investment. It really doesn't cost that much to buy and install them, so it's not going to put you out a lot of money. You'll be able to add these features to your listings so that it builds trust and shows your guests that you take their safety seriously. You should test these detectors often so you can ensure they are still working properly.

Use Proper Cybersecurity Measures

There are risks from cyberattacks, and many people do not think of this. Home network security devices will alert you of any threats or Wi-Fi attacks. You will also be able to set a limit on how many people can connect to the device. This means that if your guests invite more people to your home and connect them to your Wi-Fi, you will be able to keep tabs on them.

You can also consider getting a VPN router that does not track your online activity. This means anything your guests do will remain private and cannot be traced back to your home's Wi-Fi. This means that you will not be held liable for any of their actions. This creates privacy for them and protection for you.

Even though insurance is really important, you do not want to be put in a position where you have to use it all the time. Insurance claims can be tiresome, and property damage will cause a lot of hassle for you. This is why you need to put things in place to prevent this from happening in the first place. If you do everything in your power to ensure that your property is safe and that you've created a safe environment for your guests, then you will likely not have to deal with insurance companies very often. In the next chapter, we are going to be looking at things that need to be done before you can list your property on Airbnb.

STAGE 3

READYING YOUR PROPERTY

11

THE ULTIMATE CHECKLIST FOR ITEMS TO BUY FOR YOUR PROPERTY

New hosts that joined Airbnb since the start of the pandemic have collectively earned over $1 billion.[1] This is just the new hosts, so as you can see, it has been quite profitable even throughout a time when people traveled at a limited capacity. This being said, you need to ensure that you have everything in place in order to cater to your guests' needs. Creating checklists is going to help you in this regard. It allows you to keep tabs on what you need to provide your guests and what has run out. This ensures that you're not missing out on anything and that every guest will get the same experience.

BATHROOM(S)

- Bath Towels
- Hand Towels

- Toilet Paper
- Hand Soap
- Shampoo
- Conditioner
- Body Wash
- Toothpaste
- Floss
- Additional Toiletries
- Body Lotion
- Disposable Razors
- Disposable Toothbrushes
- Shower Caddy
- Towel Rack
- Hair Dryer
- Bath Mat
- Plunger
- Garbage Can

BEDROOM(S)

- Bed Linens
- Pillows
- Tissues
- Safe for Valuables
- Bedside Table and Lamp
- Garbage Can
- Notepad and Pen
- Hangers for Clothing
- Alarm Clock

KITCHEN

- Tea and Coffee
- Tea Kettle
- Sugar and Spices
- Dishes
- Pots and Pans
- Silverware
- Cups
- Wine Glasses
- Ice Trays
- Coasters
- Tupperware
- Cleaning Supplies
- Dishwashing Liquid
- Hand Soap
- Trash Bags
- Mop
- Broom
- Dustpan
- Oven Mitts
- Dish Towels

LIVING ROOM

- Coffee Table Reading Items (Books, Magazines, Travel Guides)
- Pens and Pencils

APPLIANCES

- Washer and Dryer
- Television
- Cable and/or Subscription Streaming Service
- Clothing Iron and Ironing Board
- Wi-Fi

SAFETY EQUIPMENT

- First Aid Kit
- Smoke Alarm and Carbon Monoxide Detector
- Fire Extinguisher
- Contact List for Emergency Services
- Wi-Fi Thermostat
- Childproofing
- Disaster Kit
- Anti-slip Mats

CLEANING SUPPLIES AND EQUIPMENT

- Cleaning Spray
- Paper Towels
- Gloves
- Duster
- Powdered Cleanser
- Magic Eraser
- Drain Cleaner

- Broom and Dustpan
- Vacuum

When it comes to listing your property on Airbnb, the small details really do matter. These are the things that will help you get those 5-star reviews. Creating a list and structure for yourself will make sure that you're not letting any of these things slip or fall through the cracks. In the next chapter, we are going to go over how to establish effective house rules so that you can ensure the safety of your property and your guests.

12

TOP 10 TIPS FOR ESTABLISHING EFFECTIVE HOUSE RULES

One of the easiest ways to keep yourself from getting into heated disputes with the guests is to set clear expectations from the start. In order to do this, you can utilize house rules. This will make sure that your guests understand exactly what you expect from them, and you can hold them accountable if they do not follow the rules.

WHAT ARE AIRBNB'S HOUSE RULES?

Your house rules are exactly what they sound like. You'll be setting rules for your guests to adhere to during their stay. This sets expectations and prevents misunderstandings. It also allows you to hold guests accountable for anything that happens. There are already some built-in house rules that are on the Airbnb platform. You can go through these and then add to them to ensure that you are covering all your bases. Some house rules are going to be specific to your type of property, while others are just going to be about general aspects of rental properties.

TOP TIPS FOR SETTING HOUSE RULES

Well-structured house rules allow both parties to understand what is to be expected. The goal is to make your rules clear and understandable for your guests. This will minimize any miscommunications and misunderstandings.

Tip #1: Be Specific and Clear

The first tip is to be specific and clear. You want to make sure that there is no room for misinterpretation. Even if it means that you have to use very simple language, try not to use any big words or unnecessary language, as this can confuse guests. You have to take into consideration that many people who are staying on your Airbnb might not be native English speakers or might not know the local terms that you use. This is why it's so important to be as simple as possible so that your rules are as clear as possible.

Tip #2: Be Reasonable

It can be very easy to go overboard with these rules. Please remember that you want guests to have fun and not feel like they are being extremely restricted. This is why it's so important to be reasonable with the rules that you set. Think about your guests' experience when you are setting the rules. Guests will look at the rules before they book, and if you have too many restrictions, they might not want to book with you. It might be a good idea to have a friend or family member look over your rules and give their opinion on them. This way, you can get an outside view of it and tweak it from there.

Tip #3: Tailor Your Rules to Your Target Guest

When you're writing your rules, take into consideration your target guest. You need to make sure that the rules are relevant to them. Try and read your rules from the point of view of your target guest. Think about whether you would appreciate all the rules or points given to you if you were in their shoes. You can remove all the irrelevant points and change your language based on who your guest is. This will help you communicate better with them and make sure that your rules are actually relevant.

Tip #4: Keep It Friendly

While it is important to be extremely clear with your rules, it is advisable to be friendly and polite as well. You don't want to come off as demanding and rude. All guests would like to be treated nicely and not be spoken to as children. Check the tone in which your rules are coming across. You can write it in a commanding tone, but remember not to be arrogant. In order to do this, you can add a few friendly touches here and there. You can add a few lines before the start of the rules list to set a friendly tone for what is to come. A guest should feel pretty comfortable when they read the rules, but also understand how important it is to do so.

Tip #5: Communicate Your House Rules Early On

From as early on as possible, make sure that your guests understand and respect the house rules. You can make it very easy for your guests to view your house rules even before they book. Once they have booked, you can email them a list of the rules along with the other information that you want to give them. Another helpful tip is to have a list of the house rules in your welcome package when the guests arrive. All of these will solidify the rules in your guests' heads and make sure that they aren't missing anything. They will already know what you expect of them before they get to your property and will be reminded of it at various intervals.

Tip #6: Keep It Concise

Once you've decided on all the important points of your house rules, you need to make sure that it's not too long and tedious to read. Each rule should be short and not consist of more than around ten words. This will allow your guests to quickly move through the rules and not feel like there's too much information to take in. Stick to one sentence for each rule. For example, instead of saying, "we highly encourage that you do not smoke on our premises as this can lead to an unpleasant experience for the next guests who arrive," you can simply say, "no smoking allowed." It is short and simple, and it gets your message across with no miscommunication.

Tip #7: Use Bullet Points

Bullet points are your friends. Bullet points make things a lot easier to read. When everything is in one long paragraph, it can be difficult for your guests to move through it. Bullet points will allow your guests to skim through the rules at a quick pace, and it just seems a lot more inviting and easier to read. It also helps them see how many rules there are at your property.

Tip #8: Prioritize Your Rules in Order of Importance

When you are creating a list of rules for your guests, make sure that they are in order of importance. As your guests read through the list, it is pretty likely that they will get bored by the time they come to the end. This is why, if you have the most important ones at the beginning, you know that these are definitely going to be the ones that are followed and taken notice of.

Tip #9: Have Your Rules Online and at the Property

Make sure your guests can access your rules online and have a physical copy at your property. If the rules are online, your guests will know what is expected of them before they get to the property. They will also be able to ask you any questions they might have about the rules. Then you can create a physical reminder for them if you have this printed out and at the property. This way, it is easy for them to have a look at them when they need to.

Tip #10: Use an Appropriate Structure

When you are writing out your rules list, make sure that you have structured it in a way that is easy for them to read and understand. You can create a poster with all the rules on it so that it is easy to understand. Feel free to add visuals to the printed copies of your rules so that they are more eye-catching and not dull. The main point about these rules is that they are easy to understand for your guests.

Establishing house rules is an important part of not only building a solid relationship with your guests but also automating your Airbnb business, so you have fewer problems to deal with in the future. It is one of the most important things you can do when you are renting out your property. In the next chapter, we'll look at using your house rules to create your house manual.

13

HOW TO CREATE YOUR HOUSE MANUAL

A simple key to setting yourself apart from other Airbnb hosts and delivering a memorable experience for your guests is providing a comprehensive house manual that thoroughly details your home. House manuals should be easy to access for your guests and provide easy-to-use instructions for everything they need. You can guarantee that your guests will have a much better experience when they understand how to use everything available on the property.

WHAT IS A HOUSE MANUAL?

You might be thinking that you do not have to create a manual because you already have the house rules. However, the house manual is something a bit different. It is basically like a how-to guide for your home. There might be things in your home that need a bit more explanation in order for your guests to understand how to use them. It will allow your guests to have a reference guide if they encounter any problems during their stay.

The house rules are basically like the do's and don'ts of your home, but the house manual shows your guests how to use things properly. You can add things to your house manual, such as how to use certain appliances, where to find amenities, and how the guests can make the most of their stay with you. The content and purpose of house rules versus house manuals are completely different. Your house manual does not show up on your Airbnb listing page. Instead, you will leave a copy of your house manual in the home when your guest checks in, and you can send a copy to them once the reservation has been confirmed.

WHAT DOES A HOUSE MANUAL LOOK LIKE?

There are many different formats in which you can structure your house manual. It really doesn't have to be rocket science, and you can definitely show your personality through it. The first thing that you're going to need is a short welcome message. This is a personal welcome message that you will write in order to establish a connection with your guests. This is especially important if you are not meeting your guests at check-in. Remember not to go overboard with your welcome message. Short and sweet is typically best. Here is an example of a good welcome message:

Dear Guest,

Welcome to [insert house name here]. We are so excited to have you stay with us!

This home is incredibly special to us, and we have made so many memories in it. We hope that you will be able to create many amazing memories as well.

Over the past few years, we have really enjoyed renting it out to travelers such as yourself. This home is a great starting point to discover the city and its surroundings. There is so much to do and see, and I'm sure you will fall in love with the city just as we have.

In this manual, you will find tons of important information. This will help you to make the most of your stay. There are instructions on how to use appliances, recommendations for delicious food places, and much more.

We truly hope that you have a magical stay!

Sincerely,

[Insert your name]

As you can see, this welcome note is personal and welcoming. It seems very friendly and shows the guest that there is a person behind the rental property. It also isn't long or drawn out because most of the information is going to be in the manual anyway.

After the welcome message, you can include some property information as well as contact information. This will be your contact info, emergency contact details, and if you are using a property manager, then include their contact details as well. You can also include the Wi-Fi password and any other codes or passwords they would need in order to utilize things in your house. This can be just after the first page so that it's easy to find.

You can attach your house rules to your manual so that everything is in one place. Then you give a general walk-through of your property's essentials. This can be how to use the various appliances so your guests understand how to operate everything in a way that is safe. This will prevent your guests from breaking anything because they are confused or simply don't understand certain aspects of your home. Even if you think it is common sense, it is really best to have these instructions. If your guests are coming from other countries, it is likely that they would do things differently and might not have the same types of appliances as you.

Other important details that you should include are check-in and check-out times. This is just a reminder because they should already know the times beforehand. If you provide parking for your guests, then include some parking information and instructions. This will prevent them from parking in a spot that obstructs other vehicles and people who live in your area. Also, include some local transport information so your guests can easily get around town. This is especially important if they are not arriving in their own car.

A page with some information about the local area is always welcome. You are the expert on the city or area in which your guests are staying. You want to ensure that they are going to have a good time, so give them a few recommendations for amazing restaurants, sightseeing spots, or local treasures. There might be things you know that are not common knowledge, and you can share this with your guests so they have a good experience and stories to tell.

You should also include an emergency page. This page will have emergency contact details for the local services around you. The fire department, police station, and other emergency services are important. It is highly unlikely that your guests would need to use these emergency services, but it is a good idea to have this information. You can also include information as to where the fire extinguisher and first aid kits are. This should be the last page of your manual, as this will make it easier for your guests to find if they do need it.

Even though this might seem like a lot of information, it really isn't. When you are structuring your manual, you will see that the information doesn't fill more than a few pages. When we think of manuals, we can think of thick books, but this should not be the case. Your guests are not going to be reading through a hundred-page document when they are on vacation. Your manual should not be more than a few pages long and just cover the necessities.

A house manual is like a comprehensive guide for living in your home. Making a detailed house manual goes a long way to helping form a clear understanding of the expectations between guests and hosts. It also allows the guest to understand how to utilize the property correctly so they have the best stay possible. In the next chapter, we will be going through legal and compliance issues you may have to consider before starting your own Airbnb business.

14

LEGAL REGULATIONS TO CONSIDER

The average host in the US earns the highest in the world per year, at over $18,000 annually.[1] In most cities and states, it is going to be easy for the average US citizen to take part in Airbnb. However, it is important to understand the legal regulations so that you don't have to pay any penalties or fees later on. This helps you to be better prepared and understand what your government requires from you in order to start an Airbnb business.

COMMON LEGAL RESTRICTIONS RELATED TO AIRBNB

When you are an Airbnb host, it is really important that you understand the laws in your city, country, state, or territory. The platform doesn't actually provide any legal advice, so it is a good idea to get this advice directly from your government or municipality. However, there are some considerations that could help you to understand the laws and regulations in your jurisdiction.

Business Licenses

There are many jurisdictions that require business owners or operators to apply for a license. You will need to do this before you can start operating your business. You will be able to find up-to-date information on this on your local government website. Most government websites have sections explaining the business licensing process and provide you with all the forms and relevant information that you will need.

Building Codes

Most governments have certain rules and regulations that specify minimum construction, design, and maintenance standards for buildings. These can also include health, safety, and habitability regulations. There are also certain rules that will apply to residential and non-residential uses of a property. Furthermore, certain jurisdictions might require that you take part in an inspection to make sure that your property meets the minimum requirements and standards. Only then will you be able to utilize your property as an Airbnb. Not all jurisdictions or areas will have such strict rules, so it is important to know what applies to you by going on the government website or contacting your local government.

Zoning Rules

There could be many rules or laws that dictate how you use your home. These can be found in a zoning code, city ordinance, or planning code. You can consult these rules and regulations to find out if your listing is consistent with the current requirements or uses definitions.

Special Permits

You might be required to get a special permit in order to rent out your home. You'll need to contact your local government or municipality to see if this applies to you. You will also be able to get some information on how you can get this permit.

Tax Laws

Most states and jurisdictions will require an Airbnb host to collect tax for each stay. You will then need to pay this tax to the city or to the jurisdiction where it applies. There are certain jurisdictions where Airbnb will automatically collect and remit certain taxes on your behalf. You will need to find out if this applies to you so that you have the relevant tax information.

Landlord-Tenant Laws

If you are hosting longer stays, you might be subject to landlord-tenant laws. This varies by jurisdiction and may impose more strict legal obligations on you and provide your guests with additional legal rights. It is a good idea to consult a lawyer that specializes in landlord-tenant law in order to learn more and see what applies to you.

WHERE TO LOOK FOR APPLICABLE LAWS AND REGULATIONS

The laws and regulations can seem a bit confusing, but it is quite easy to get the information that you need in order to make the right decisions going forward. You can log on to the Airbnb help center and see what kind of regulations apply to your city. This might not provide all the information you need, but it can provide a guideline.

If you are in North America, then you will most likely be required to obtain permits and business licenses before you can operate your Airbnb. The exact requirements will vary depending on many different factors. You can start off by going onto your local government website to see what kind of permits or licenses you would need in order to start a short-term rental business. In most cases, you will find a comprehensive guide and the steps that you need to take in order to obtain the permits. You would likely be able to fill out all the forms you need online and then submit them. If you are confused, you can call your government offices and see if they can help you with any of your queries.

Once you have determined exactly what permits and documents you need in order to start your business, you need to make sure that your property is in compliance. Each location will have its own safety regulations for the tenants. If you need to make any renovations or improvements to your property, then do so. Also, obtain proper insurance to ensure your guests' and your safety. You will also need to make sure that you comply with any requirements your insurance company might have in order to insure you for certain things.

It is so important that you consult your local laws and rules to make sure that you are not violating any regulations when you start an Airbnb. It is better to seek clarification and ask as many questions as possible, rather than assume that everything is going to be fine in the end. You don't want to be struck down with heavy fines, end up being sued, or possibly end up being evicted just because of a technicality that could have been avoided. Rather, do all the necessary homework now so that you can avoid any unpleasant situations in the future. In the next chapter, we are going to be talking about keeping your property clean and well-maintained in order to get those 5-star reviews.

15

A CLEAN PROPERTY LEADS TO 5-STAR REVIEWS

Many negative reviews come from the fact that the property has not been cleaned properly or is unkempt and untidy. Your guests might stay at an amazing property with beautiful amenities, but if it is not clean, they are going to complain. Would you like to stay in a hotel or guest house that is not clean? We all have higher standards of cleanliness when we are paying for a vacation rental. This means that you have to put a lot of emphasis on making sure your property is clean and neat.

TURNING OVER YOUR PROPERTY

Cleaning your property between stays is called turning over the property. It is not just about doing a quick clean and then welcoming the next guest. When your guests check in, you want them to feel that they are in an absolutely pristine boutique hotel. When you are doing a turnover cleaning, it is going to require a bit more energy and work than a regular house cleaning. It is a good idea to clean up your property as soon as your guest leaves. This will allow you time to discover if there are any damages or problems so you can process a claim as soon as possible. If there are any damaged items or items that need to be replaced, you have time to do this before the next guest arrives.

Turning over your property requires consistency. You need to create a system for yourself so that each guest gets the exact same experience. This actually makes it a lot easier, and you'll find that you can turn over your property a lot quicker as time goes on. It's a good idea to use a checklist so that you understand what needs to be cleaned and you don't miss anything. Later on in this chapter, we are going to give you an example of a checklist that you can use and tweak depending on your property.

Many first-time hosts underestimate the amount of time they need to clean their property. Of course, the size of your property definitely comes into play when it comes to how long you will spend cleaning. When your guests check out, you will only have a specific amount of time in order to clean it and get it ready for the next guest. You should have at least a four- or five-hour cleaning window so that you can do things thoroughly and make sure that everything is up to standard.

You might have to consider hiring a cleaner if you are not going to be available to turn over the property or if the work is going to be too much for you to handle on your own. If you are going to hire a professional team, make sure that you have cleaned your own property before and know exactly what needs to be done. This allows you to set the standard so you can communicate effectively with your team about what they need to get done. You will then need to provide them with a checklist as well so that the standard remains consistent.

It is also important that you do a thorough inspection when you are turning over the property. A guest might have broken something, or there might have been some sort of malfunction.

It is a good idea to test all the appliances and the plug points to make sure that everything is still working fine. Also, check through the glassware and other commonly used items to make sure that nothing is chipped or broken. It is a good idea to bring a few extras with you when you come to turn over your property. You will need to replace anything that is broken so that the next guest gets a good experience.

REMEMBER TO RESTOCK AND RESTAGE

The turnover time also needs to include restocking and restaging your property. As your guests use your property, things are going to be moved around and finished. You need to make sure that you have reverted the property back to default settings so that your next guests are able to enjoy it just the same. Using the checklist that was given to you in Chapter 11 is a great starting point. Make sure that you bring all the items that could be used up with you. Things like toilet paper, shampoo, conditioner, tissues, and pantry items, will all need to be replaced. If you have these with you, then it's going to make it a lot easier for you to simply replace them. You can take any extras back to your storage.

Restaging simply means moving all the furniture and other items back to how they were before your guests checked in. It is a good idea to take a few pictures of your ideal property setting. This way, you can use the picture as a reference when you are moving everything back. It'll make things a lot easier until you are used to restaging your property. When you are cleaning, it is going to be a good idea to move the furniture so you can get underneath, just in case your guests have dropped things or lost things under the furniture. Then you can move things back into the ideal position.

Have a look at your decor items and make sure that they are all clean and in the proper position. When guests stay at a property, they might move things like artwork, decor, and similar items. You can simply wipe them down and move them back to where they are supposed to be. Since you are restaging for the next guest, candles are a good idea to add some ambiance to your property. Check to see that all the candles are not completely burned down or finished. You can replace them as needed. If you have any other disposable decor items, then you can also replace these and make sure that they are in the right position.

Your guests are going to expect the property to look like the listing photos. This is why it is so important to make sure that you are resetting your property to how it was in those photos. If you have cleaners that are working for you, then make sure they have access to these photos so they have a reference to how the furniture and settings should look.

Your guests' welcome package is something that you're going to have to restock every time. You can actually create a few welcome packages and keep them with you. This way you can just replace the old ones each time you turn over the property. You can provide these to your cleaners and your property managers so they can do the same for you.

CREATE A CHECKLIST

A checklist is really helpful to make sure that you are providing each guest with the exact same service. Here is an example of a housekeeping and turnover checklist that you can use on your own Airbnb.

Kitchen:

- Wash and put away the dishes.
- Wipe and sanitize all surfaces.
- Wipe and disinfect sink and backsplash.
- Clean inside and outside of fridge, freezer, and oven.
- Wipe down all small appliances like coffee maker and microwave.
- Refill all kitchen cleaning supplies like dish soap and sponges.

- Clean windows and dust the windowsills.
- Mop the floor.
- Take out trash, clean the garbage can, and put a fresh trash bag in.
- Ensure all kitchen supplies are arranged nicely.

Bedrooms:

- Remove sheets, pillowcases, blankets, and mattress protectors. Make sure they are laundered properly.
- Wipe down all surfaces including ceiling fans and decor.
- Remove smudges from windows and mirrors.
- Disinfect high-touch items like remotes and light switches.
- Check for any personal belongings that have been left behind.
- Check for damage on furniture and bedding.
- Vacuum the floors.
- Empty trash cans.
- Restock with fresh linen.
- Remake the bed with a clean and fresh set of bedding.
- Arrange all decor and artwork correctly.

Bathrooms:

- Remove all dirty towels and bath mats; have them laundered correctly.
- Look in the drawers and cabinets for any personal items left behind.

- Wipe down mirrors and windows.
- Disinfect countertops, sinks, faucets, and backsplashes.
- Scrub down the bathtubs and showers.
- Clean and sanitize the toilets thoroughly.
- Dust all windowsills, fans, and vents.
- Sweep and mop the floors.
- Replace and refill all amenities such as hand soap and toilet paper.
- Check bathroom for signs of wear and tear and damage.
- Place clean towels and bathmats appropriately.
- Ensure all the bathroom items are arranged neatly.

Living Room:

- Wipe down all tables, shelving, and furniture.
- Dust appliances such as the TV and radio, as well as decor.
- Wipe down windows, doors, and windowsills.
- Dust lighting fixtures such as lamps and ceiling fans.
- Sanitize frequently touched items like light switches and remotes.
- Wipe down and refresh couches, throw pillows, and chairs.
- Launder any blankets and replace them with new ones.
- Sweep and mop or vacuum the floors and carpets.
- Ensure any additional items such as books, board games, decor, or art are arranged neatly.
- Arrange throw pillows and blankets neatly on the couch.

Dining Room:

- Wipe down tables and chairs; make sure there are no crumbs in any hard-to-reach places.
- Check underneath table to make sure there is nothing stuck underneath it.
- Wash tablecloths and runners.
- Clean centerpieces.
- Wipe down all decor and replace in appropriate areas.

Outdoor Areas:

- Remove any branches and dead leaves from the lawn.
- Ensure all the bushes are trimmed and neat.
- Remove any debris or weeds.
- Wipe down all outdoor furniture.
- Clean railings.
- Sweep the patio or deck.

Laundry:

- Check for clothes left behind in the washing machine or dryer.
- Clean out any washing detergent left in the washing machine compartment.
- Wipe down all surfaces.

It is so important that you take the time to turn over your property correctly. If you have a look through Airbnb reviews, you will see that one of the most common things that people complain about is cleanliness. You can easily get marked down two or three points just because your property is not clean. In chapter 16, we will be moving on to setting up your booking system.

YOUR SECRET SUPERPOWER AS AN AIRBNB OWNER

If you have knowledge, let others light their candles in it.

— MARGARET FULLER

In Chapter 25, we're going to look at the power of good reviews – and how you can get them. Think back to the last time you booked travel accommodation for yourself. I'd hazard a guess that reviews are one of the first things you looked at. Although we'll delve into this in more detail later on, it's worth having in the back of your mind at all times that positive reviews are your secret superpower as an Airbnb owner... which is why I'm planting this seed in your mind now.

Your property is a place people want to feel safe and comfortable while they're away from home, so it's clear that reviews are going to be very important for you. They let other travelers know exactly what they're getting for their money, what their experience will be like, and ultimately, whether they're making the right choice for them. Positive reviews give customers faith in your property and influence their decision to book.

I want to help other business owners like you because I truly believe Airbnb can be a lucrative and fulfilling business for anyone – and reviews are just as important for authors as they are for business owners. So, as you might have guessed by now, I'd like to ask for your help.

Simply by leaving your honest review of this book on Amazon, you can help the Airbnb business remain the goldmine it is today.

Just as reviews tell guests which property is right for them, they tell readers which books will provide them with the information they need. As a result, more business owners like you will see success... and *that's* how Airbnb will remain the lucrative business it is today, serving you and your fellow hosts well into the future.

Thank you for taking the time to help me here – and I hope it illustrates just how important those reviews are going to be for you. Keep reading to find out more!

Scan this QR code and leave a brief review on Amazon.

STAGE 4

SETTING UP AND MANAGING BOOKINGS

16

BOOKING POLICIES TO CONSIDER

Before you can even think about creating your listing on Airbnb, it is important to give some thought to the policies you want to enforce for guests staying on the property. Thinking about these things before actually publishing your listing helps you to be prepared, and eliminates any unnecessary issues down the line. Prevention of problems is always better when it comes to dealing with other people. This will be a lot less stressful for you and your guests. It will also help your guests to understand exactly what is expected from them.

COMMON BOOKING POLICIES THAT GUESTS ASK ABOUT

When you're running a short-term rental property, there are a few booking policies that guests are going to be concerned about. The Airbnb platform allows space for you to communicate what your booking policies are like so that it is clear and your guests understand it from the get-go.

Cancellation Policy

The first kind of policy that we are going to be talking about is the cancellation policy. It is also arguably one of the most important policies that you should think about. The Airbnb platform gives you a few options to choose from, and this is all going to be based on your preferences and what you deem as the best fit for you. These are the most commonly used policies.

Flexible Cancellation

The flexible cancellation policy allows your guests to cancel their booking and get a full refund up until 24 hours prior to check-in. In that case, you won't get paid. If they cancel after that, you will be paid for every night they stay plus one additional night.

Many guests like the flexible cancellation policy because it allows them to get a full refund. With this being said, it might not benefit you as it is difficult to find somebody who wants to book in their place within a day. When the cancellation can be done so close to the actual check-in time, it might result in you losing money. This is definitely something to think about when you are renting out your Airbnb.

Moderate Cancellation

A moderate cancellation policy allows the guest to cancel the booking and get a full refund up to 5 days before check-in. If the guest cancels after this, you will be paid for every night they do stay plus an additional night. You will also get 50 percent for all unspent nights. Using this kind of cancellation policy allows you to have a bit more security and it holds the guest a bit more accountable. They will not be able to cancel and get a full refund unless they cancel at least 5 days in advance. This might give you some extra time to find someone else to book in their place and still make money.

Strict Cancellation

A strict cancellation policy will allow your guests to receive a full refund if they cancel within the first 48 hours after they have made the booking. This needs to be at least 14 days prior to check-in. If the guest cancels between 7 and 14 days before check-in they will receive a 50 percent refund on the nightly rate, but will not be refunded for the service fee. If they cancel within 7 days of arrival, there is no refund. A strict cancellation policy means that if a guest books with you, they need to be sure that they can stick to the commitment. The issue with this type of policy is that it can put a lot of guests off. They might not want to book too far in advance just in case they have to cancel, and this means they would be looking for another property that would be a bit more flexible.

If you are new to running your own Airbnb, then it might not be a good idea to have this kind of cancellation policy. Since you have not yet built up your reputation and probably don't have that many reviews, there is no guarantee for your guests that your property is going to be worth it. As you build up your reputation and more people start to know you and your property, it would be a better time to implement this kind of cancellation policy. Properties that are very popular and have back-to-back bookings tend to do better with this kind of cancellation policy because people will do their best to ensure that they get a spot and keep the commitment to this day.

Flexible Long-Term Cancellation

If you are going to rent out your property on a long-term basis, 28 days or longer, it overrides the standard cancellation policy. The guest would need to cancel 30 days prior to check-in in order to receive a full refund. If they cancel after this time has elapsed, you will receive full payment for the nights they stay and for an additional 30 nights. If fewer than 30 days remain on the initial reservation, you will be paid for all remaining nights. This is done to protect you, as a host, since you will find it very difficult to find a new guest for a long-term stay in a short period of time.

Super Strict Cancellation

The super strict policy is not available to every host. Only experienced hosts who Airbnb has invited can select this option. There are also two options: super strict for 30 days and super strict for 60 days. The 30-day option means that if a guest cancels at least 30 days before check-in they will receive 50 percent of the total nightly rate. The service fee is non-refundable. If you choose the 60-day option, the guest would need to cancel 60 days before check-in to receive a 50 percent refund on the total nightly rate. The service fee for this option is also not refundable.

Non-refundable Option

If you are concerned about guests canceling their booking, you can set up a non-refundable policy. To do this, you would need to offer a discount of 10% off your base rate. Guests can then choose under which policy they book with you. If they choose the discounted rate, the booking will be non-refundable, and in case of a cancellation, you will get paid for all nights booked. The reservation will be subject to your cancellation policy if they choose the standard rate.

Cleaning Fees

There is an option to add a cleaning fee on top of your regular nightly rate. This helps with expenses that will go toward the maintenance and upkeep of the property. Guests will see the total that will include the cleaning fee as they browse through the site. When they get the bill, the fees will be listed separately, so your guests will know exactly what they are paying for. Bear in mind that if the cleaning fee brings up the total nightly stay price significantly, this might deter a few guests from wanting to stay with you.

Security Deposit

Airbnb will not charge a security deposit. Instead, Airbnb will inform every guest at the time of booking that they may be charged if they cause any damage throughout their stay, although there is one exception. You can still charge guests a security deposit if you manage your listing with API-connected software. It is completely up to you whether or not you want to charge a security deposit, but if you are worried that your guests may damage or break something, it is a good idea. It helps keep the guests accountable for your property because they know that they will not get their money back if they damage something.

Over and above your house rules, there are other booking policies you'll need to consider and decide on prior to publishing your listing. Thinking about these policies is really important because it helps protect you and your property. It also allows the guest to understand exactly what is expected of them so that there are no miscommunications and misunderstandings. The policies have been put in place to help the hosts keep themselves and their properties safe and in good condition. In the next chapter, we will go over effective pricing strategies for your Airbnb listing.

17

THE PRICE IS RIGHT—STRATEGIES FOR MAXIMIZING PROFITS AND INCOME

The average price per night for an Airbnb around the globe in 2021 was $137. In the US, the average was $208 per night.[1] This is due to multiple factors, but as you can see, the US Airbnb market brings in quite a bit more money. You need to understand how to price your property well to bring in the most amount of money. Your pricing strategy really does matter because this will either help you to maximize your profits or end up not working for you at all.

HOW TO FIGURE OUT YOUR AIRBNB PRICING STRATEGY

Airbnb hosts are always trying to figure out how much their place is worth. I'm sure you want to be able to make the most amount of money from your Airbnb rental. In order to do this, you need to understand how much people are willing to pay for your property. You do not want to underprice your property.

Even though you might get a lot of bookings, you will be losing out on money. You also don't want to overprice your property, because then people will be turned off from booking with you.

It is a good idea to have a look at your competition to see what they are charging. This way, you can get a good idea of what people are willing to pay in a similar area and for a similar property with the same types of amenities. When you are researching your competition, it is a good idea to put together at least six similar listings and take note of different types of information. You will want to record rates for the weekdays in the low season, the high season, weekends in the low season, and weekends in the high season. All of these will have different prices because of what people will be willing to pay for each. This is why it is important to not just "set it and forget it" when it comes to your pricing. A dynamic pricing strategy will allow you to attract more guests and maximize your profit.

You also want to check out the pricing on peak dates. School holidays and public holidays such as Christmas, New Year, and Easter will be priced higher because there will be more demand. Special events like local sporting events, concerts, and conferences will also attract more people to your area and this means the pricing will go up. If you live in an area that has seasonal work like harvesting, prices tend to go up as well. Basically, anything that's going to draw people to your area who will need accommodation is going to drive up the general market price of an Airbnb stay. This means that you will be able to charge a bit more for your nightly rates since the demand is going to be higher.

EFFECTIVE AIRBNB PRICING STRATEGIES

There are multiple Airbnb pricing strategies out there. You will need to pick the one that's going to work best for you and ensure that you make the most money from your pricing strategy. Maximizing your profit means that you have more money left over to enjoy, and you will also have more money to invest back into your Airbnb if you choose to do so.

Maximum Fill Rate Strategy

The first strategy is called the maximum fill rate strategy. In order to implement this strategy, you will need to follow along with your competitors' pricing. You need to attempt to offer the best experience in your city or area. The main goal is to ensure that you have the maximum occupancy rate that you can have. This means that you will need to offer even more value than your competitors in your region. You will then set your nightly rate slightly lower than average to continuously attract guests. Even though your nightly rate is going to be lower than average, your income will be pretty stable since people would rather choose your property over another property that is similar but charges more.

Maximum Rate per Night Strategy

For this strategy, you will be setting a higher rate for your nightly charges. This will allow you to increase your net profit from each individual booking. You should expect that the number of bookings will be fewer because not everybody will want to book at this higher rate. However, your income will be sufficient because you will be getting a maximum profit from the least amount of effort possible. Your occupancy rate will be lower than average but you can look at this as an advantage because you're dealing with fewer guests and will have to spend less time and money turning over the property. It is important not to go overboard with this kind of strategy, as it could lead to nobody wanting to book with you. You also have to ensure that you are in an area where people want to book. If you are in a remote area and people are not interested in booking in that area or there is not a lot of demand, this strategy is going to be very difficult to implement.

Long-Term Rental Strategy

Another strategy that you could implement is the long-term rental strategy. In order to do this, you will be setting your pricing according to long-term rentals, which means monthly rates instead of nightly rates. You will likely need to provide a rental agreement and conduct a house tour before confirming the booking. It is a lot more work beforehand because you have to do additional paperwork as well as promote your listing a bit more than just on Airbnb. However, once you have found somebody who is going to stay at your property for a longer period of time, you can be completely hands-off for the most part. You will not have to turn over your house until the rental period has elapsed. So it ends up being a lot less work for you in that sense.

You will also have a much more stable income because you will be paid per month rather than nightly. You will have to take into consideration that you will have to bring down the monthly rate so that it is manageable for people to pay. While people might be happy to pay $200 per night if they are staying for a long weekend, they are definitely not going to be happy to pay $6,000 for a 30-day stay.

Balanced Airbnb Pricing Strategy

This type of pricing strategy is an integrated strategy. You will combine all three pricing strategies that we have already mentioned in order to efficiently manage your Airbnb business. This is more of a dynamic approach, so you will not just be leaving your price stagnant. You will continuously be changing your pricing strategy according to the demand and the season you are in. For example, in seasons where the demand is not high, you can choose to employ a long-term rental strategy so that you reduce the risk of leaving your property vacant. Then, during seasons where the demand increases, you can use the maximum fill rate or maximum nightly charge strategy to ensure that you get a maximum profit.

The Flexible Strategy

A flexible strategy is one way you will determine how much you will be charging for different seasons and different dates. This is also called a "dynamic pricing strategy" because it's always changing. One option that is available on Airbnb is the smart pricing tool. This sets your rates based on the current market. Many people like to use this tool, and there is definitely some appeal because it means that it is less work for you. However, it can end up losing you money since it is an algorithm that sets the price and not you. If you understand the market that you are in, it is going to be better and more profitable for you to focus on your own pricing strategy.

The flexible strategy that I am going to mention now is one that I have implemented in my own Airbnb business and had amazing results from it. The highest-yielding exercise is going to be to fill up your weekdays. This can be tricky, especially in the low seasons. In order to do this, you are going to need to drop your prices from Sunday through Thursday, if they are not already booked. You will need to drop your prices in order to get bookings at the start of this pricing strategy. I know it can be hard to drop your pricing because you've put a lot of work into your Airbnb and want to get paid fairly for it. However, being tied to the nightly rate as the overall value of your property is a mentality that will not allow you to increase your income. Your goal should be the bigger picture and you should look at ways to make more money annually rather than just focusing on how much you'll be making each night.

Let's look at an example to show you how you can utilize this kind of strategy to earn a lot more money over a 4-week period than just focusing on a nightly rate. Let's say your rate is set at $350 per night. This would be on your weekends, so Friday and Saturday, and you booked out all 4 weekend dates, so 8 nights. Let's also say you booked 8 nights on the weekdays at a rate of $250 per night. Let's calculate your earnings:

	Nights Booked	Average Nightly Rate	Total Earnings
Weekdays (Sun to Thu)	8	$250	$2,000
Weekends (Fri to Sat)	8	$350	$2,800
Total	16		$4,800

Now that you have your earnings for the month, you can calculate how many nights you're not booked. This will help you to see that the rates that you had were not successful for those days. In this example, you would've missed out on 12 weekday nights and no weekend nights. So your missed earnings would be calculated as follows:

	Nights Not Booked	Average Nightly Rate	Total Missed Earnings
Weekdays (Sun to Thu)	12	$250	$3,000
Weekends (Fri to Sat)	0	$350	$0
Total	12		$3,000

Now that you have this information, you need to calculate how many nights you could have booked and what rate would have worked. Now, it is not realistic to believe that you can get 100 percent occupancy throughout the year. Let's estimate it instead at about 80 percent occupancy. You would then need to discount 80 percent of the nights that were not booked. We can discount these nights up by 50 percent so that you can get 80 percent of them booked out. 80 percent would be ten nights.

	Nights Not Booked at 80% Capacity	Average Nightly Rate at 50% Discount	Total Earnings
Weekdays (Sun to Thu)	10	$125	$1,250
Weekends (Fri to Sat)	0	$350	$0
Total	10		$1,250

By reducing the rates, you were able to increase the number of bookings and get 80 percent of your available dates booked. This means that instead of not getting any income on those days, you have now made an additional $1,250 in the month. Most people do not want to do this because they would lose out on the full rates on the discounted night. This is actually completely true. This is why you should not discount your rates if the dates are far out. You should only discount your rate as the dates start creeping closer and they're still not booked out. When dates are far away, you can keep your rates higher so that you can make the most amount of money from fewer dates. As you get closer to the dates and you see that your desired occupancy is not being reached, this is when you start thinking about discounting your rates. Your discounted rate will start getting booked up a lot quicker so that you can make that additional money. It is much better to have your property occupied at a discounted rate rather than not have it occupied at all.

Another benefit to discounting your Airbnb is that you are getting more guests into your property. If a guest really enjoys staying at your property, they are likely to want to come back. They might not mind paying an increased amount of money for a weekend stay. They might also recommend your property to their friends and family, and this will improve your reputation as well as the number of people that are staying with you. As you can see, running an Airbnb is about a lot more than simply setting a nightly rate. You have to be willing to change up your strategies and look into the long term as well.

ONLINE TOOLS

There are so many helpful online tools available to you that make things a lot easier. If you utilize these tools, you will find that creating pricing strategies becomes a lot easier. You'll have access to a lot more information than if you just rely on your own physical research. You might find it helpful to try out a few tools to see which one works best for you. Here's a list of some to do some additional research on:

- Wheelhouse
- Beyond Pricing
- PriceLabs
- Host Tools

Finding the right pricing strategy for your Airbnb can be really tricky. Picking the right one depends on multiple factors that are constantly changing. Making use of software tools can really help you to adjust and optimize your price to maximize your earnings. You also should think about adopting a dynamic pricing strategy rather than just setting one price and leaving it there. Doing this will allow you to increase the amount of income you make per month. In the next chapter, we will take a closer look at how you can deliver a smooth and effortless booking experience for your guests.

18

STREAMLINING THE BOOKING PROCESS—HOW TO FIND GREAT GUESTS

Over 500 million guests stay in Airbnbs every year. In order to capitalize on the number of people that are willing to stay at Airbnbs you need to be able to streamline your booking process and find the right guests. There are certain tweaks that you can make in order to optimize your online booking experience for your guests. This will help you to avoid any horror stories happening to you.

WHAT IS INSTANT BOOK?

There is a feature on Airbnb called Instant Book. You can choose to select it or not, depending on what you prefer. If you choose to use it, then it will remove the approval process for you. Typically, a guest will request to book with you, and this will then be sent to you for approval. You can do some research on the guest and find out whether you want to approve this booking or not. Once you have approved it, the booking process will continue and payment can be made. This process can take a bit longer for the guest because you might want to find out more about them, their dates, and other situations. If you turn on Instant Book, the customer is completely in control. This will apply to all available nights in your calendar and they will be able to book as long as they have met the requirements that you've already ticked off.

Selecting the Instant Book option really does make your life easier because it is one less thing that you have to do. It also makes the guests' lives a lot easier because they can make bookings quickly. If they have a delayed flight or an emergency trip somewhere, they can simply book for the next day and know that their booking will be quickly confirmed. Guests who like this will use the filter on Airbnb so they can find Instant Book properties. You also increase your chance of getting the Superhost status because, in order to get this badge, you will need a 90 percent response rate. Your chances of achieving this are much higher with the Instant Book option.

On the downside, it removes the barrier between you and your guest. This means that you are giving up some control and don't really know who is walking through the front door. If you are not too concerned about this, then Instant Book could be a really great feature for you. If you are a new listing, then Instant Book can really help you. Your goal as a new Airbnb owner is to get as many people to book with you as possible. If you remove as many barriers as possible, then your chances of people booking with you increase. You will also show up on the Instant Book filter so that you have more guests interested in your property. With this being said, when you have the Instant Book option set up, you will need to be prepared for anything. Somebody could book today and arrive tomorrow, or even book to arrive at your property five hours from now. This option typically works better if you live close to your property or have property managers who are there to handle your Airbnb. You will also need to ensure that your property is always ready to receive guests because you simply do not know when they are going to walk through the door.

HOW TO SCREEN GUESTS WHEN THEY INSTANT BOOK

It is still a good idea to do some sort of screening even when your Instant Book option is on. The good news is that you can set conditions under which guests can book with you. For example, you can choose to only accept guests who have provided a government ID or who have been recommended by other hosts on the platform. This means that the guests have been pre-screened, and there is more information about them available. People who have ID verification on their accounts are a lot more reliable than those who do not. It also shows that they have used the platform a few times, so they are aware of the process and the etiquette that is involved with Airbnb.

It is also a good idea to have a look at the guests who have booked, even if the Instant Book function is on. You can still look through their social media and Airbnb profile to ensure that they are reliable. This will help you to have peace of mind and be prepared for whoever comes walking through your door.

STORY TIME

When you are an Airbnb host, you can't have full control over your guests and what they will be like. Even if you do extremely strict reviews, you might still end up with a bad one. On the other end of the spectrum, there are so many stories of people who have accepted guests that have no reviews on their profiles and they have been amazing. Sometimes it is just the luck of the draw and it is the risk that you take when you are running an Airbnb.

A few years ago, I decided to turn on my Instant Book function. This was just on a trial basis to see if my bookings increased. I noticed that for one of my listings I would receive last-minute bookings every now and then. The guests wanted to arrive within a few hours of booking. Once I saw this, I figured out that I may be missing out on many more of these bookings if people only search for listings that have Instant Book activated. This led me to turn on Instant Book, and I never looked back.

My last-minute bookings increased for this listing by a huge margin. I also decided to stop lowering my rates at the last minute in order to attract more people. This was because I knew that, come 5 p.m., someone would make a reservation to arrive very shortly after. In fact, I decided to increase my rate and just focus on the last-minute traveler demographic—I tried the strategy with another one of my properties, but I didn't see any positive results. For that property, I decided to leave the

Instant Book function off. I learned that Instant Book doesn't work for all properties. However, if you are in a location where lots of travelers are booking at the last minute, give it a trial run. For my Instant Book property, I had around 25 percent of people who didn't have any reviews. This was either because they were new to Airbnb or they were not regular users. Personally, I cannot recall a single instance where a guest who didn't have any reviews caused me any trouble. With this being said, I know of friends who are renting on Airbnb and have had very different experiences.

All the positive experiences I had with my guests prompted me to write some glowing reviews for them. Here are a few examples of the reviews I left:

> *Stacy and her friends came to stay over at my property for the weekend. They left it in great shape and even did a good cleanup of the place. It was an amazing experience hosting them, and I would definitely recommend them to other hosts.*
>
> *Walter was an amazing guest. He communicated effectively throughout the process. I was incredibly happy to host him and his fiancée. Both of them treated the place with the utmost respect, and it would honestly be a pleasure to host them again.*

The names of the guests have been changed here, but I think you get the point. These are just a few of the examples of great reviews that I left for Instant Book guests. This just goes to show you that it is definitely possible to have an amazing guest experience even if you do not get to approve them before they book with you.

With all of that said, it is important that you have a balanced view of what can happen with Airbnb. I'm going to share the stories, not to scare you, but to make you aware. You might even have a few laughs along the way. The truth is that becoming an Airbnb host is truly a journey and an experience like no other. You really don't know what kind of people you are going to meet, and even in the moment, if you have to deal with a horrible guest, it could always turn into a funny story that you can tell later on. This is not to make light of any of the bad experiences that people have gone through, but to simply reframe them in a way that is not completely negative. When you start off with any kind of business, you need to expect that there will be a risk of something bad happening. Have a look at these two stories and hopefully find some humor in them.

Justin was fairly new to running his own Airbnb, so he was quite open to allowing any kind of guest to book with him. There was a guest who wanted to pay cash rather than use the website system. In hindsight, this should definitely have been a red flag, but Justin just wanted to make some extra money. He did a quick Google search of the guest's name and discovered that this person was actually a high-profile escort. It was too late to cancel the booking because the guest had booked with the Instant Book function for that evening. All Justin could do was wait it out and see what the property looked like the next day. Once he arrived at his property, he was met with empty wine bottles all over the floor, condom wrappers in the bin, and a whole host of other gross things. Let's just say that Justin was a lot more careful about who he let into his property from that day on. He also got the entire place deep-cleaned. Good choice, Justin!

Cory Tschogl simply wanted to rent out her property in Palm Springs, and two brothers decided to rent it for six weeks. Everything seemed normal, and the booking process went quite smoothly. However, a big surprise took place when it was time for them to check out. These two brothers simply refused to move out of the property. They decided to cite California's tenant rights, which makes it a lot more difficult to evict them after 30 days (remember we spoke about this in an earlier chapter?). There was a lot of publicity on the story, and with the help of a couple of lawyers, they left after two months and didn't leave any damage. However, Airbnb did offer to pick up the legal fees, which was pretty decent of them, I must say.

Finding great guests for your Airbnb starts with doing some specific research on who you want to attract to your property. I've already gone over how important it is to choose a target audience and target market so that you can construct your Airbnb experience around that type of guest. This is also going to help you with the booking process. The people who would be interested in your property would most likely be those who fit into your target market. It'll make it a lot easier for you to understand who is going to be booking with you and allow you to be a bit more trusting to use the Instant Book option. You should also ensure that you are investing some time into screening your potential guests so that you can filter out any problematic people. Even if you are screening your guests to the tee, you might still get a few unpleasant ones. It is best to mentally prepare for this so that you understand how to handle them if the situations do occur. If you follow a good process from the start, then you will lessen the likelihood of any of these negative experiences actually happening to you. This is why every step of the process is so important. In the next chapter, we are going to look at how you can use a channel manager to help manage bookings.

19

RENTAL CHANNEL MANAGERS

While Airbnb may be one of the more popular online vacation rental sites, there are at least a dozen other sites where Airbnb business owners can list their properties and gain more exposure. It actually makes a lot of sense to use multiple platforms in order to broaden your potential customer base. This will result in you getting more bookings for your property.

WHAT IS A CHANNEL MANAGER?

While advertising a property across multiple different platforms might sound like an amazing idea, it is not as simple as that. When you list properties on different sites, you have to be able to manage this property. The risk of double-booking is definitely high since the platforms are not all connected. This is where the channel managers come in. A channel manager is basically a software platform that makes it incredibly easy for a host to manage rental listings across a number of different platforms. They will be able to do this from one interface, so it makes life a lot easier for the host.

Not every host is going to benefit from using a channel manager. One thing you have to take into account is that this is a paid service. So you need to make sure that it's going to be beneficial to you before you sign up for one. The type of host that would benefit from a channel manager would be somebody who is managing their listings across various different platforms. It definitely does help to increase your exposure and minimize the risk of double-booking when you are doing this. It also allows you to communicate with your guests in an easy way, as you don't have to keep switching between multiple platforms. On the other hand, if you are a host who is perfectly happy with just using the Airbnb platform, there's no need to get a channel manager.

WHAT TO LOOK FOR IN CHANNEL MANAGER SOFTWARE

Not all channel managers are created equal. There are definitely some scams out there, so you need to make sure that when you invest in good channel manager software, that it is legit. The first thing you need to do is make sure that it is from a legitimate company. You can find this out by doing a Google search and seeing what people are saying about the software. The more people that are talking about it, the more likely you can trust the company. Have a look at the company's website and ensure that it looks reputable. You should also have a look to see if they are official Airbnb partners. You can do this by going onto the Airbnb website and checking out the software partners. If the system that you were looking into is not on the list, then there's a good chance that the technology is weak and it's probably not going to be of great benefit to you.

You can also visit a software evaluation website like Capterra to find reviews from past and current customers. This is a really good way to find out what people like and don't like about certain software. This will help you to make a more informed decision. If the channel manager software that you are looking into comes from a company that is integrated with a bigger booking website such as Airbnb, Booking.com, TripAdvisor, or Vrbo, then you know it's a good option.

Top Channel Manager Software Options

There are many different channel manager software packages out there. It is definitely worth it to do your research to find out which one is going to be best for you. To get you started, here is a list of the top channel manager software options:

- Avantio
- Hospitable
- Hostaway
- Hosthub
- iGMS
- Lodgify
- OwnerRez
- Rentals United
- SiteMinder

- Uplisting
- Zeevou

One way to help you scale up your Airbnb business or maximize occupancy for a listing is to use a channel manager. This can help you to get your listing on many other rental platforms that are similar to Airbnb. Getting more exposure is always a good thing because it means an increase in revenue. You will also get your name out there on multiple different platforms so people will recognize you and your property. In the next chapter, we will start looking at what goes into high-performing listings. This way, you can start to replicate that in your own business.

STAGE 5

GETTING NOTICED

20

HOW TO CREATE YOUR FIRST AIRBNB LISTING

Nobody counts the number of ads you run; they just remember the impression you make.

— BILL BERNBACH

HOW TO LIST ON AIRBNB

Understanding how to list your Airbnb property on the website is really important. The good news is that it is pretty easy to do so. The platform basically guides you through the whole process as you progress. This means that it is incredibly user-friendly and you are not likely to mess up or miss any important information.

The first step is going to be to create your account. Once this is done, you can start to add your listing. You will select the "add a listing" option that's on the top right corner of the homepage. From here, you will be directed to a form that you will need to fill in with the general criteria of your property including:

- **Home type**: This is basically whether your property is an entire place, a private room, or a shared room. We have already discussed this in detail, so you should know the type of property that you have.
- **Number of guests**: This is the maximum number of people that can be accommodated by your listing.
- **City**: This one is pretty self-explanatory. Once you select your city, Airbnb will give you an estimate of what you can expect to earn per month based on the information you have already provided.

Once you have filled in all of this, you can click over to the next part of the process. On this page, you need to provide some specific details about your listing and property. You will be given a selection of descriptions to choose from, and you will choose the most accurate type. Then you'll have to further specify the description from a drop-down menu. As you move along in this process, you will be guided to add more information about your listing, including things like the address, amenities, number of beds, and number of bathrooms. This is quite a lengthy list of things that you are going to need to check off, but make sure that you are choosing the right options. You will be able to edit it once you are finished, so you don't have to stress about it being final.

You will also need to include high-quality photos, a description, and an amazing title. We are going to get more in-depth into these things in the later chapters, so for now, just know that these are things that are required of you. Make sure that you are filling out your profile completely so that your guests have as much information available to them as possible. This makes you seem a lot more trustworthy and you'll definitely get a lot more bookings and interested guests for your property.

OTHER SHORT-TERM RENTAL PLATFORMS

As I mentioned before, there are plenty of other short-term rental platforms that you can use. You can definitely do some in-depth research on these different platforms to see what they offer and if you would like to list your property on them. I'm going to give you a quick overview of the best ones so that you can understand them better.

Vrbo

This stands for vacation rental by owner. It only offers apartments and private homes, so if you have other types of properties, you would not be able to use this platform. If you list your property here, then you will also be listed on Expedia since there was an acquisition that brought them all under the same umbrella company.

Vrbo works on a 5 percent booking fee plus a 3 percent credit card processing fee. The policies that deal with cancellation and payment will vary depending on the property. One thing to note is that a host is unable to delete any reviews, whether they are negative or positive.

Booking.com

Booking.com is definitely a guest-friendly and easy-to-navigate platform. There's also an instant book option, just as there is on Airbnb. Since guests enjoy using the platform, it is quite a good option for you to increase your occupancy rate. There are more flexible cancellation options, which also encourages its use. Additionally, there are no booking fees for users. One thing to note is that there is a 15 percent host fee on all completed bookings for most hosts. The fee can vary slightly depending on location, so it is best to check this out for yourself. This will be charged upon the guest's arrival, so if there is a cancellation or if the guest does not show up, then the fee will not be charged.

Expedia

This is typically not the first vacation rental platform that comes to a guest's mind. This platform seems to be overlooked by hosts, but this can actually be an advantage because you can get ahead of the competition. When you list your property on this platform, it will also appear on a few other travel sites. You will be paying a 15 percent fee on each booking. Last-minute bookings are also available on the site, and things like flights and car rentals are all in one place, which makes it very convenient for guests who are looking for the best deals.

TripAdvisor

One of the most prominent features of this platform is the ability to provide feedback from the travel community. Guests love using this platform to search for places to stay. Since it was founded in 2000, a huge number of reviews have been collected. This means that most travelers will trust it. All property listings will be translated across 26 languages and appear on all 26 TripAdvisor sites. This definitely helps expand your reach so you can attract more travelers from international locations.

The host fee per booking on this platform is 3 percent. This is on the total rent, which includes any optional fees or required fees that have been specified for the property. The guest can also book car rentals and flights through the platform, which makes it very user-friendly and a favorite amongst tourists from all over the world.

Creating a listing on Airbnb is an incredibly straightforward process. It doesn't take too much work and it's really difficult to mess it up. The platform makes sure that the process is easy to follow and the prompts allow the user to be guided through the process step-by-step. There are definitely similar processes that are involved with other short-term rental platforms. Some are better than others, so it is a good idea to do trials with these platforms so you can get a better feel for them. In the next chapter, we are going to be looking at what you should optimize in your listing to get the best chance of attracting guests on Airbnb.

21

HOW TO OPTIMIZE YOUR LISTING TO MAXIMIZE BOOKINGS AND INCOME

You cannot get anybody to do something if they're not paying attention to you.

— BRIAN CARTER

HOW TO RANK ON THE FIRST PAGE SEO

Airbnb SEO will determine your position among other listings with the same search results. You want to be able to get to the top of the page so more people will recognize you and book with you. Think of it like Google. When you search for something on Google, you are far more likely to click on the websites that are listed on the first and second pages. Anything after that usually calls for a new search to be typed in the search bar so you can find something that you truly are looking for. The same thing happens with the Airbnb platform. If you are ranked at the top, you will definitely get more bookings because more people will see you. The good news is that there are plenty of things that you can do to improve your SEO ranking.

Getting Back to Guests Quickly

The first thing that the platform is going to take into account is how quickly you respond to your guests. There are a few metrics that are used to measure your response to potential guests. Your response rate is the percentage of inquiries that you have responded to within a 24-hour period. Your response time indicates the average amount of time that it takes you to respond to each new message. These metrics will be based on data from the previous 30 days.

One thing you can do to help yourself out is to have a few common responses typed out. Most guests will ask very similar questions so this is a really good tip to help you feel less overwhelmed and so that you can spend less time typing. All you need to do is paste the relevant answer or guidance and send.

Avoid Cancellations

In order to be in the algorithm's good books, you need to avoid any kind of cancellations. You can do this by ensuring that your calendar is updated so you can reduce the chances of having to cancel on someone. Rejections also play into this, so you need to be sure that you are only rejecting people if absolutely necessary. The platform will compare you to other hosts, so you just need to make sure that you are not rejecting more guests than other hosts.

Enable Instant Booking

By now, you already know all the benefits and technicalities that come with Instant Book. At the end of the day, using the Instant Book option means that the Airbnb platform will push your listing to the top.

Leverage Your Top Reviews

Getting good reviews: It's so important to rank high on the Airbnb SEO. It will look at how many guests you've hosted and then how many have left ratings. You want to be able to get the best reviews possible but the good news is that a few bad reviews won't really affect your ranking if you have a lot of good ones. After your guests have stayed with you, why not email them and ask them for any feedback to improve your service. If they come back with positive reviews then you can also review them on the platform in a positive light. If they have given you negative feedback and are not happy with the stay then do not review them.

Optimize Photos

Taking good photos is really important to improving your Airbnb SEO. We are going to talk more about this subject in a later chapter, so hold on tight.

Choose a Great Title

The importance of your title cannot be underestimated. This is what's going to grab your guests' attention, so it needs to be good. There is a whole chapter dedicated to this because it is so important.

Write an Excellent Description

Your description is such an important part of your Airbnb listing. It is what allows your guests to understand what you offer and if you use the right type of words then the Airbnb SEO will push you to the top. We also have an entire chapter dedicated to this since it is such an important topic to cover.

Use Social Media

You can help get more interaction with your Airbnb profile if you post on your other social media platforms. Not only that, but Airbnb will notice this and boost your rankings immediately. Any kind of external link is very useful to help you climb in the search results.

Update Your Airbnb Profile

If your host profile is updated and complete, then you are more likely to rank well with Airbnb SEO. The host looks more trustworthy when the profile is up to date and all the information is filled out.

Showing up at the top of the Airbnb search results is a matter of fine-tuning your listing and getting every detail right. You will not regret doing this because there are so many benefits to ranking high with the Airbnb SEO. You'll be able to get more visibility and therefore get more bookings. In the next chapter, we will go into more detail about how to get attractive photos for your property.

22

HOW TO CAPTURE ATTRACTIVE PHOTOS OF YOUR PROPERTY

In one study, better quality photos lead to a 17.5 percent increase in bookings. This simple statistic shows how important taking good quality photos is. At the end of the day, most guests will not be able to take a tour of your property before they book with you. The photos are the only things that they will be able to use as a reference for what they will be paying for.

GETTING A PROFESSIONAL VS. SHOOTING YOUR OWN PHOTOS

One thing you should consider is getting a professional to take some quality photos of your property. This is an expense that you will have to consider, but you should think of it more as an investment. When you have professional photos taken, it will make you stand out from the crowd. Your property will look so much better than the other properties that are listed. You will look a lot more professional and like you truly care about putting your best foot forward. This says a lot about you and it builds trust with your potential guests.

You have about eight seconds to grab the attention of your potential guests. This number is even lower for the younger generations. This is really not a lot of time to make an impression. This is why having exceptional photographs is so important. You need to utilize that eight seconds of attention to work for you. Having professional photos taken will allow you to showcase your home in the best possible way. There is a lot of knowledge that comes with a professional photographer, and they will know exactly how to highlight the best features of your property. Things like lighting and angles can be difficult to understand, so a professional is a good option.

You might also be able to set a higher price if you have better quality photos. Listings that have photos that have been taken by professionals can command a premium of around 26 percent higher than listings that don't have this. Even though hiring a professional photographer is an upfront cost, it would likely make up for this with the number of bookings you get and by being able to charge a bit more than your competitors because your property simply looks better.

TIPS FOR TAKING AMAZING PICTURES OF YOUR PROPERTY

If you have decided that hiring a professional photographer is not for you, then there are a few things that you can do to enhance your photos. It is really important that you take the best photos that you possibly can. It is possible to get really good quality photos by using a smartphone that has a good quality camera and by implementing the tips that we are going to be speaking about now.

Organize and Tidy Everything Before You Shoot Photos

When you take your photographs, you need to put your best foot forward. This means that you need to clean and declutter your entire property. Make sure that everything is organized exactly the way you want the guests to see your property. Do your best to make things beautiful and ensure that there isn't too much clutter in the pictures.

Prep and Inspect Rooms Beforehand

Before you plan on taking pictures, ensure that you have prepared each room and that it has been inspected. You should do this even if you are hiring a professional photographer. This will just make everything go a lot smoother. You can use the checklists that have been provided for you in the previous chapters to help you prepare your home as if a guest is arriving the next day.

Use Natural Sunlight Where Available

There is just something about natural light that makes everything look 100 times better. This is why you need to prepare to shoot your photos in natural daylight. Natural light will help to enhance your property and increase the contrast, depth, and colors of your photos. Make sure that all of your blinds and curtains are completely open to allow the natural light to flow in. You should also switch on all your lights, even in the daytime. This will prevent any shadows or dark corners from showing up.

Shoot into a Corner

This might seem like a strange tip, but it is much better to face your camera toward a corner than down a straight wall. The corners will add some dimension to your photo, and you will get a much bigger space in the picture. Your room will look a lot more inviting and open. Test it out for yourself and you'll be able to see the difference.

Look at All the Small Details

The small details truly matter when it comes to your pictures. It's so easy to get caught up with all the big items and major amenities, but the smaller things could be make or break. The little things are what complete the picture for the guests, so do consider these things. Your property should be filled with personality and make your guests feel welcome. Try not to make it look too clinical; otherwise, it's not going to be very appealing.

Use Panoramic Shots

Using panoramic shots is one of the best ways to show off your entire room in one photo. If you are unable to take a panoramic picture, then try using a wide-angle lens. This will give the guests a better idea of the size of the space.

Try Different Angles and Perspectives

Taking pictures from just one angle is going to look very one-dimensional and boring. Guests will not want to scroll through 100 pictures that are taken from the exact same perspective.

Add some variety by changing up the angles every now and then.

Use Post-editing Software

There are so many different photo editing software and apps out there. Many of them are completely free and will help you enhance your pictures. You can use these apps or software to crop and edit your photos to make them look their best. Small adjustments can really help make your pictures stand out.

If you can't afford a professional photographer or would rather take photos yourself, there are so many things that you can do to help you take amazing pictures. Just make sure that you are implementing as many tips as you possibly can. Your pictures are really important for the guests to get a true idea of what your property has to offer. In the next chapter, we are talking about how to write compelling listing titles.

23

LISTING TITLES THAT GET CLICKS

Lots of Airbnb hosts make the mistake of overlooking the title of the listing. The problem with this approach is that they're not focusing on what every guest is going to see when they find the listing: The title! It is one of the first impressions that your guests will get of your property, and that's why it's so important. It also helps the guest understand what your property is all about and what it provides. Remember, you only have about eight seconds to make an impression, so a catchy title is really important. If you have a good title, then you will have a better chance of a guest clicking on your listing and then converting that into a booking.

SECRET TIPS AND FORMULAS FOR WRITING TITLES THAT INCREASE BOOKINGS

There are many tips and tricks that can help you write an eye-catching title. The payoff is going to be huge when your title really draws in the guest.

Secret 1: Focus on What Makes Your Property Unique

You want a title to stand out from the crowd, so make sure that you focus on what makes your property unique. Use descriptions and adjectives that highlight the unique aspects of your properties. If you have a pool, make sure this is in your title because it's something different. Perhaps your property is in an interesting location or it has an amenity that guests are looking for. These unique features can be added to a title so guests know exactly what you are offering them.

Secret 2: Take Up All 50 Characters in the Title

Airbnb allows up to 50 characters in a title. Make sure to use up all of these characters so you can give an accurate description of the property. With this being said, there has been an update to the guidelines. Even though you are still able to use all 50 characters, only 32 characters will appear on mobile phones. This means that the first 32 characters are going to be the most important. Most guests will be searching using their phones because it is just simpler.

Secret 3: Be Specific with Your Words

Generic words simply don't get you anywhere. If you are too vague, you will just get lost in the crowd. Try and choose words that are unique and really speak to your property and describe it properly. You don't want to use words that people have never heard before, but you want to make sure that you are avoiding words like "nice," "good," and "pretty." Even though these words are technically descriptive words, they basically tell you nothing about the property. Since you only have a limited number of characters to use in your title, you should make sure that you are utilizing them well.

Secret 4: Name Your Property

A really cool thing to do is to name your property something unique. Instead of referring to it as a house or apartment, you can give it a distinctive name. The name of your property should be descriptive and provide an insight into what it is. It also speaks to your target guest so that you can grab their attention.

Secret 5: Tailor It to Your Audience

You want your target audience to be grabbed by your title. This is why you need to understand who your target guests are and then tailor your title to them. If your target audience is couples who are going for romantic getaways, then you can make your description more romantic and describe it in a way that's going to appeal to that group of people. If you are targeting large families with small children, then you can make your title more fun and family-friendly.

Secret 6: Use Abbreviations Where Possible

Since you have only a limited number of characters to use, it is wise to utilize abbreviations where possible. Just remember that the abbreviations you use should be ones that people actually understand. You don't want your guests to be completely confused about what you are trying to say.

Secret 7: Stick to Proven Title Formulas

There are a few formulas that help you create very effective titles. These ones have been proven time and time again. It will allow you to draw attention to your listing and also convey accurate information that the guest wants to know.

- Formula 1: [Specific Adjective] [Property Type] w/ [Unique Features]
- Formula 2: [Specific Adjective] [Property Type] Perfect for [Experience Type]
- Formula 3: [Adjective] [Property Type] Near [Landmark]—[Distance]
- Formula 4: Enjoy [Unique Feature] at [Specific Adjective] [Property Type] in [Location]

Your listing title might seem like such a small thing or a minor detail, but it is one of the first things that your guests will come across. This means that you want to make sure your title gets them to click and hopefully book with you. In the next chapter, we are going to talk about what makes for a perfect listing description.

24

WRITING LISTING DESCRIPTIONS THAT MAKE GUESTS INSTANTLY BOOK WITH YOU

If a strong title is what catches your guests' attention, then a powerful description is what gets them to book with you. The description is not a place for you to simply summarize your listing. It is an opportunity for you to sell your guests on why they should book and stay at your property over the other options they have. You want to highlight the most significant and unique features and benefits of your property and convince them to stay with you. This should be your top priority. Writing a good description is something that can truly get you many more bookings.

WHAT MAKES A LISTING DESCRIPTION EFFECTIVE?

In order for your description to be effective, it needs to draw the attention of your guests. Instead of being too salesy and sounding like a car salesman, you need to tell a story. Something that's going to make the guests want to continue reading to find out what else your property has to offer. Your description also has to be eye-catching. Something that makes guests want to learn more about your property. This is why it shouldn't be a sales pitch but rather an effective description.

Now, it can be easy to get carried away when you are describing your property. Just make sure that you are being accurate and telling the truth. Stretching the truth in your description is not going to be of any benefit to you. Sure, you might get the booking, but when they come to your property, they will see that it does not match the description. This will result in you getting negative reviews, and you just don't want that.

Your description needs to be targeted and tailored to your target audience. This is why it is so important for you to know who your target audience is. The way you would describe something to a family looking to go on vacation is completely different from the way you would describe something to a businessperson coming into town for a meeting. Regardless of who your target audience is, your description needs to be easy to read. People do not want to read lengthy descriptions of things that aren't going anywhere. Make sure that it is specific and concise but still conveys the message you are trying to get across. Try not to use language that is too complicated for people to read through. It's really not going to benefit you if your guests can't even understand the words that you are using in your description.

THE BASIC STRUCTURE OF A TOP-PERFORMING DESCRIPTION

You can follow a basic structure in order to create a great description. Here are a few things that you should definitely include in your description:

- Interesting introduction.
- Description of all the rooms.
- Describe outdoor spaces.
- Discuss the location and nearby attractions.

Your main goal when writing your description is going to be to answer the questions before your guests even ask them. A few things that guests would like to know about are as follows:

- How close is your property to the nearest landmarks and public transportation?
- How many rooms, beds, and bathrooms are available on the property?
- Is the property kid-friendly and what is the pet policy?
- What are the unique features of your property that others do not have?
- What amenities and items do you provide?
- What is available in the surrounding areas and some things to do?

People will likely skim through the description and not read it word for word. This is why it is a good idea to segment the description into separate sections. You can use paragraphs and bullet points for this. You will start off with the introduction, then in the next paragraph, you can move into the different living spaces. You can use bullet points to describe the amenities you provide. Then in the final paragraph, you can review the general location and sign off. You can also use headings within your description so that you can break up the different sections. This does make it a lot easier to read, and your guests will be able to easily find the information they are looking for.

AN EXAMPLE OF HIGH-PERFORMING DESCRIPTIONS

Title: Newly Renovated Romantic House with Ocean Views

What You Will Love

- Complete renovation was done in 2022, so everything is brand new.
- Breezy coastal decor.
- Gourmet, fully equipped kitchen with stainless steel appliances.
- Beach access is just one block away.
- Private outdoor space with barbecue.
- Beautiful deck to enjoy the ocean views.
- Can use as a remote workstation with Wi-Fi.

About the Property

This beautiful house is steps away from the gorgeous coastline, so you can smell the salty air every time you take a breath. It is located in a peaceful area, so you will not be disturbed when you enjoy your morning coffee on the deck.

The lounge and living spaces display works by local artists and coastal decor that has been designed by local woodworkers. With three bedrooms and two full bathrooms, there is space to comfortably accommodate six people. The primary bedroom has a king bed and an en suite bath. The second bedroom also offers a king, and the third, a queen. Both of these bedrooms will share a large bathroom situated in the hallway.

The outdoor amenities are simply spectacular. With a large deck that offers a lounge and dining area, you can enjoy breakfast, lunch, and dinner with views of the ocean and the sound of the waves crashing against the shore. Feel free to sit out on the deck in the evening with a glass of your favorite wine and gaze over the ocean or stargaze to your heart's content.

Getting to Know the Area

The property is conveniently located close to many natural amenities. You are steps away from the ocean and just a short walk away from a beautiful recreational park. A stunning golf course is a simple five-minute drive away.

The town is an artist's paradise with art galleries, spas, boutiques, and restaurants. You will find craft beer, farm-to-table cuisine, and delicious cocktails around every corner. The town draws all manner of explorers, so if you are looking to meet some interesting people, then one of the many bars is the place to go.

This is simply a tiny treasure of the region that everyone will come to love and enjoy. There is truly something for everyone, and it draws you in with its quiet and charming vibe.

25

THE POWER OF WORD OF MOUTH —GETTING PROFITABLE REVIEWS

Without integrity, no company can have positive word of mouth.

— JAY ABRAHAM

TIPS FOR GETTING TOP-RATED REVIEWS FROM GUESTS

Getting good reviews is incredibly important when you're running your own Airbnb business. Reviews mean credibility. People are far more willing to book with hosts who have a lot of positive reviews. It shows that people have been happy with the service that they received and are willing to come back. This is one of the best ways to increase your revenue and bring in more guests. With this being said, it can be quite tricky to get these good reviews when you're first starting out. However, there are many things that you can do to get these reviews and ensure that they are good ones.

Tip #1: Underpromise and Overdeliver

The first step to getting amazing reviews is to exceed your guests' expectations. This means that you need to underpromise and overdeliver. Now, there is definitely a balance to this because you still need to convince your guests to book with you. So if you are too humble with your descriptions and your title then you will not get any bookings. The key is to deliver what you promised and then a little bit more.

Your guests' expectations are going to be set by what you have mentioned in your listing. If you provide something that is even better than that, they will be delighted. It's all about adding something special and a bit different. You don't have to change around your whole property, so the guests are completely shocked when they walk through the door. In fact, this is probably a bad idea. Instead, look at a few small things that you can do that will be a happy surprise to your guests. For example, include a welcome note in your welcome basket with a few local snacks and suggestions of where they can go to enjoy their stay. This is a small cost to you, but it leaves a huge impression.

If there are any pitfalls at your property, ensure that you let the guests know about this in advance. You can mention it in your listing but frame it in a slightly positive way. For example, if the street on which your property is located can be quite loud in the mornings, you should mention it in the listing. If you don't mention it and you get a guest who is a light sleeper, they will absolutely hate the experience and give you a negative review. If you put this in the listing, they will have already expected this and the light sleeper would probably not have booked with you in the first place. This is just better for everybody involved.

Tip #2: 6-Star Service Leads to 5-Star Results

You should do your best to go the extra mile for your guests. Start thinking about how you would like to be treated on your own property. The things you would like to have done for you are the things you should provide for your guests. Perhaps you can contact them a few days before they arrive and ask if they have any special requests. You can also follow up with them during longer stays and ask if they would like a complimentary cleaning service.

Tip #3: Pick the Right Guests to Stay with You

Making sure you pick the right guests is so important. One of the biggest reasons hosts should background check their potential guests is to see their ratings and identify whether it is a good choice to allow them onto their properties. If you see that other hosts have enjoyed the guests, then there is a good chance that these are good people.

Tip #4: Take Care of Issues Right When They Happen

It is very common for issues to arise when a guest stays at a property. Even if you have meticulously planned things down to the tee, slipups sometimes happen. In many cases, it's not even going to be your fault. If some of these incidents do happen, don't panic. All you have to do is handle them as soon as possible. Most guests are not too worried if something small happens, they just want to know that the issue will be resolved quickly.

It really does help if you have procedures and steps in place to help you address any potential issues quickly. For example, if you know that power cuts occur in your neighborhood, then have a plan to mitigate this issue. You can also notify guests of common issues that might occur and how they can go about dealing with them. As long as you provide them with the resources to deal with any potential problems, they will usually be OK with it.

With all of this being said, you must remember that the guest will always be right. If they come to you with an issue, it needs to be resolved, even if you don't think it's a big deal. Guests will be coming from all different places and backgrounds. This means their standards are going to be different from yours. Being gracious with your guests is a good way to establish a relationship with them and ensure that their needs are met. If you want to get good reviews from your guests, then you need to take care of them in the way that they want to be taken care of. You must show them that you are on their side, and whatever the problem is, make sure that you apologize sincerely and take action as quickly as possible. You will definitely see this pay off in your guest reviews.

Tip #5: Try to Be Flexible with Things Like Check-In Times

Being flexible with your check-in and check-out times is a good way to get good reviews. Guests really do appreciate it when they can arrive and leave whenever they please. Sometimes plans simply do not go according to plan, and it is not possible to check in at the regular time. Perhaps a guest has arrived earlier than expected or is going to arrive much later. Having a flexible check-in time allows the guests to set their own schedules for what is going to be best for them.

The best way to implement this is to have electric locks, so your guests won't have to arrive only when you can let them in. You can set a personal code for the guest, and they can use this to unlock the doors. This is actually an added safety measure because it can be set to lock automatically after a certain period of time and it will prevent guests from losing their keys or leaving your home unlocked when they go out. A cheaper option would be a key safe lock box if electric locks are not possible. You can place the key in the box and set a code to open it so the guests have access to the key. Since you don't have to be there when they check in, it allows you to have more flexibility as well.

Tip #6: Overcommunicate

Communication is key when you are dealing with other people. It is much better to overcommunicate than to undercommunicate. Your guests are going to be dependent on you for a good experience. This is especially so if they are new to the area or have not used the Airbnb platform before. It is a good idea to be accessible to your guests so they can contact you if they have any questions or need a helping hand. Remember, it can be scary to be in a place that you do not know or are unfamiliar with. Having somebody that you can communicate with really puts you at ease.

With this being said, it can be quite inconvenient to have somebody call you for simple things. This is why it's important to predict any common issues that might arise in your home. If you know you have a very old type of coffee machine that guests could have trouble using, stick some instructions next to it or include it in your house manual. This way, your guests will have all the information they need and they will not need to call you unnecessarily.

Tip #7: Stay on Top of Upkeep

Maintenance issues can cause an undesirable experience for the guest, and this is not going to lead to a good review. This is why it is a good idea for you to take some time to turn over the property and ensure that everything is still working well. It only takes a few minutes to do a quick scan of the property to ensure that everything is as it should be. You should also schedule inspections every now and then to ensure that all of your plumbing and electronics are working well. This way, you won't be surprised by any issues down the line because you've already taken preventative measures.

Tip #8: Keep It Seasonally Themed

Different seasons will bring out different aspects of your property and the location in which you are. If you decorate your property according to the theme, it will really bring out the best in the location. You can pull the theme from the outdoors and bring it indoors. For example, in the winter you can turn your property into a cozy feeling place. In most cases, people love to feel warm and cozy when it is cold outside. In the summertime, you can go for more fun and coastal decorations to bring a summer vibe to your property. It is no secret that every season brings its own feelings and vibes to an area. You can use this to add an extra level to your property.

Tip #9: *Seek Out Feedback from Guests*

Getting your guests' input is the best way for you to continuously improve your services and your property. Your guests know exactly what they expect and what you are missing. Most guests are very happy to give you some constructive feedback so you can make things better. Once guests have checked out, consider sending them an email to get some feedback from them. If the feedback you received is positive, then you can go ahead and ask them to leave a review for you. If you have received some negative feedback, then you don't necessarily have to prompt them to give you a review. Also, let them know that you are going to do your best to implement the feedback that they have given, so the next time they come to your property they will have a better time.

Getting 5-star reviews is a simple matter of being diligent and conscientious as an Airbnb host. Understanding what your guests need is so important to their overall experience and to make sure that you are becoming the best host that you can be. In the next chapter, we are going to touch on what it takes to create the ultimate guest experience.

STAGE 6

BUILDING RELATIONSHIPS WITH YOUR GUESTS

20 ESSENTIAL QUALITIES OF EVERY SUCCESSFUL AIRBNB BUSINESS OWNER

Strive not to be a success, but rather to be of value.

— ALBERT EINSTEIN

20 QUALITIES OF SUCCESSFUL AIRBNB BUSINESS OWNERS

We have already spoken about all of these qualities throughout the book. This is more to remind you of the qualities that you can work on. You'll be able to find information about most of these tips throughout the book, so feel free to go back and find the information that you're looking for. More likely, you will be reminded of what you have already learned so it is solidified in your brain. You will also realize that every step of the process makes you a better host. These 20 qualities are things you already know based on what you have learned.

1. Invest in high-quality photos of your property.
2. Have enough time to devote to being an effective and attentive property manager.
3. Create lasting first impressions, especially at the start.
4. Personalize every guest's experience.
5. Be as prompt as possible when responding to customers.
6. Buy back your time by outsourcing smaller tasks.
7. Success is in the details.
8. Be willing to go above and beyond.
9. Reach out personally before your guests arrive.
10. Offer some guidance for the local area.
11. Add a personal touch to every interaction.
12. Decorate your space tastefully and thoughtfully.
13. Don't overcomplicate the process.
14. Always be clean.
15. Keep supplies stocked.
16. Leave snacks for guests.
17. Price yourself competitively against hotels in the areas, not just competitors.
18. Always abide by your local laws.
19. Proactively collect 5-star reviews.
20. Don't think, just do it.

Arguably, anyone can become an Airbnb host. But there are only a select number of hosts that are able to deliver top-notch experiences that have guests constantly raving about them. This is the type of host that you should strive to become. In the next chapter, we will look at ways to automate the booking process to make operations for both you and your guests more efficient.

27

WHEN AND HOW TO USE AUTOMATION FOR YOUR AIRBNB RENTAL

Automation has been regularly shown to increase efficiency in companies across industries. For example, setting up automated processes in your Airbnb business can increase occupancy rates by as much as 80 percent.[1] That is a big payoff for reducing the amount of work that you have to do.

THE BENEFITS OF AUTOMATING YOUR AIRBNB BUSINESS

Running an Airbnb rental, or just a rental property in general, requires an investment of both time and money. If you have a busy life or you have multiple Airbnb properties, then it is a good idea to start thinking about automation as an option. As you scale your business, you will need to free up your own time because you simply can't be everywhere at once. In most businesses, automation is something that they integrate, and the rental industry shouldn't be any different.

There are plenty of benefits that come with Airbnb automation. Firstly, you will be able to work remotely and still have control over your properties. This gives you flexibility and saves you time. Routine tasks that can be automated mean that you do not have to spend time doing them. You can allocate your extra time to more important things in your business and your personal life. You'll also be able to take on more work because the smaller things have been taken care of.

Automation means that everything will run a lot more efficiently and you can increase your revenue because of this. You'll be able to speed up communication with your guests, the booking process, and cleaning procedures. Automation allows you to scale and grow your business without complicating anything. There are many different ways in which you can automate your business, and we are going to go through a few of them.

Smart Home Automation

Smart home technology is the way to go. You can invest in things like smart locks, smart televisions, and noise monitoring systems. If you have smart locks on your property, then you do not need to be there in person in order to do key exchanges or to welcome your guests to the property. All of these things can be done by themselves, and all you need to do is give your guest a unique access code. Smart TVs are just a really good way to simplify the check-in process. Anybody can figure out the smart TV, and you can schedule a welcome video to play as soon as they walk in or switch on the TV. Noise monitoring is a great way to go if you have fussy neighbors. You will be notified if noise levels exceed a reasonable level and can take action to ensure that all parties are happy.

Guest Communications

Communicating with your guests is of the utmost importance when it comes to renting out your property. You need to make sure that your guests are always kept in the loop, and there are things that they will need to be reminded about. If you have a lot of guests staying in your various properties, then it can become overwhelming to try and keep in contact with all of them. You can automate this by setting up automated messaging, automated notifications, and an email welcome series. All of this allows the guest to have the communication they need, but you are not doing anything.

Pricing Strategy

We have gone quite in-depth about pricing strategy in a previous chapter. From there, you know that it can get a bit complicated. This is where pricing strategy tools can be incredibly helpful to you. You can use dynamic pricing tools and automated pricing to help you out if you do not have the time to sit and manually work on your own pricing.

Automated Task Management

If you are not the one who is performing maintenance or cleaning services at your property, then having an automated task management service is a really good choice. This will automatically notify your cleaning service when the guests have checked out. Then they can come in and turn over the property for the next guest. Maintenance contractors can also be alerted when repairs need to be made to certain aspects of the house.

You do not have to be involved in any of this, and you know that your home is going to be well taken care of.

A Channel Management Solution

We have already gone quite in-depth with channel management services, but these are also a great way to automate many different aspects of your property management. Things like promotion, distribution, and booking of your listings can be handled across multiple platforms all from one window. This simplifies everything for you so that you are not jumping from platform to platform.

You might not yet be at a point where automation is necessary for your business. However, it's never too early to start thinking about ways you can make your operations more efficient so you can spend your time on more important things and get back some of your free time.

CONCLUSION

Getting into the Airbnb business is truly a journey like no other. You are creating a way for yourself to make extra income while doing something that is really enjoyable. You open up your home or property to other people so that they can have some amazing experiences. Not only that, but you are also creating a way to make more money and possibly start a business so you no longer have to work your regular 9-to-5 job.

By now, you should have a good grasp of what you can expect from the process. You will also be able to put together a workable strategy so that you can move forward. At the end of the day, none of the information that you have learned from this book is going to be of any use unless you start implementing it. I would suggest that you start from the beginning and slowly work your way through the book. See where you can begin implementing things to make your current Airbnb business better or start on this journey from scratch.

I would urge you to commit to taking some sort of action. This could be in the form of research or writing out a list or plan. The more you take action, the more momentum you will build for yourself. Once you have reviewed everything in the book about two times, it will be time to start going through each phase of the Airbnb framework. You can start by performing a market analysis. From here, you can just continue to take action. You will start to see things take shape the more you make moves in the right direction.

If you have found the information in this book useful and valuable in your Airbnb journey, would you consider leaving me a review? This will really help me connect with more people to help them achieve their Airbnb dreams.

Scan this QR code and leave a brief review on Amazon.

REFERENCES

Airbnb Automation: 7 Ways To Put Your Business on Autopilot. (2021, June 01). iGMS. https://www.igms.com/automate-airbnb/

Airbnb hosting: 6 ways to protect yourself and stay within the law. (2019, May 13). LearnBNB. https://learnbnb.com/airbnb-hosting-laws/

Airbnb house rules: Actionable tips and templates. (2020, September 7). Hospitable. https://hospitable.com/airbnb-house-rules/

Airbnb pricing strategy. (n.d.). Renting Your Place. http://rentingyourplace.com/airbnb-101/pricing/

Airbnb rules: 6-step checklist to stay within the law. (2019, November 27). iGMS. https://www.igms.com/airbnb-rules/

Airbnb SEO: 10 proven tips to boost your ranking. (2020, February 28). iGMS. https://www.igms.com/airbnb-seo/#

Airbnb statistics. (2022, May 4). iPropertyManagement. https://ipropertymanagement.com/research/airbnb-statistics

Airbnb supplies: A complete checklist for hosts to help you exceed your guests' expectations. (2018, October 16). iGMS. https://www.igms.com/airbnb-supplies/#

Airbnb titles: Proven formulas that attract 5x more bookings. (2020, April 27). iGMS. https://www.igms.com/airbnb-titles/

Arrojado, C. (2022, May 11). *Frank Lloyd Wright homes, farm stays, glamping sites—Airbnb's new search categories feature these cool listings.* AFAR. https://www.afar.com/magazine/airbnb-unveils-56-new-vacation-rental-categories

Average Airbnb prices by city: How much should you charge for your Airbnb? [2022] (2022, May 2). AllTheRooms. https://www.alltherooms.com/analytics/average-airbnb-prices-by-city/

Best Airbnb listing descriptions: Our top examples. (2022, March 9). GuestReady. https://www.guestready.com/blog/best-airbnb-descriptions-examples/

The best Airbnb pricing tools in 2022—maximize your profits with dynamic pricing. (2022, July 9). Floorspace. https://www.getfloorspace.com/best-airbnb-pricing-tools/

Best vacation rental channel managers 2022. (n.d.). Hostaway. https://www.hostaway.com/best-vacation-rental-channel-managers/

Carville, O. (2021, June 15). *Airbnb is spending millions of dollars to make night-*

mares go away. Bloomberg. https://www.bloomberg.com/news/features/2021-06-15/airbnb-spends-millions-making-nightmares-at-live-anywhere-rentals-go-away

Clark, R. (2021, October 28). *15 Airbnb horror stories you won't believe are true.* Lodgify. https://www.lodgify.com/blog/airbnb-horror-stories/

Clarkson, A. (2021, January 12). *Airbnb cleaning checklist | 5-star turnover success.* Mamma Mode. https://mammamode.com/airbnb-cleaning-checklist-5-star-turnover-success/

Comprehensive list of Airbnb host expenses. (2020, December 1). Unbound Investor. https://www.unboundinvestor.com/comprehensive-list-of-airbnb-host-expenses/

Daly, A. (2021, March 12). *25 insanely useful Airbnb tips that will make you a better host.* BuzzFeed. https://www.buzzfeed.com/anniedaly/pro-tips-from-airbnb-superhosts

Dar, S. (2022, February 23). *What kind of insurance do you need for an Airbnb property?* Baselane. https://www.baselane.com/resources/what-kind-of-insurance-do-you-need-for-an-airbnb-property/

Davis, G. B. (2022, June 27). *How to be an Airbnb host: 14 tips for fast success.* SparkRental. https://sparkrental.com/airbnb-host/

Deane, S. (2022, January 4). *2022 Airbnb statistics: Usage, demographics, and revenue growth.* Stratos Jet Charters Inc. https://www.stratosjets.com/blog/airbnb-statistics/

Debunking Airbnb myths | Top 10 Airbnb hosting misconceptions. (n.d.). Hostaway. https://www.hostaway.com/airbnb-hosting-misconceptions/

Deciding to list your place on Airbnb—legality and regulations to consider. (2022, July 18). Padlifter. https://padlifter.com/free-tips-and-resources/deciding-to-list-your-place-on-airbnb/airbnb-legality-and-regulations-to-consider/

Dendinou, J. (2021a, August 20). *How to a create a listing on Airbnb.* Hosthub. https://www.hosthub.com/guides/how-to-create-a-listing-on-airbnb/

Dendinou, J. (2021b, August 20). *How to create a listing on booking.com.* Hosthub. https://www.hosthub.com/guides/how-to-create-a-listing-on-booking-com/

Drew, R. (2022, June 13). *21 critical Airbnb house rules examples (& templates) for hosts.* Rental Recon. https://www.rentalrecon.com/host-advice-and-ideas/airbnb-house-rules/

Duckworth, P. (2018, October 7). *Private room vs entire place.* Bnb Duck. https://bnbduck.com/airbnb-private-room-vs-entire-place/

Filippousi, M. (n.d.). *How to write an awesome description for your Airbnb listing.* Hosthub. https://www.hosthub.com/blog/how-to-write-an-awesome-description-for-your-airbnb-listing/

5 tips to earning a 5-star review on Airbnb. (2019, December 11). LearnBNB. https://learnbnb.com/earning-a-5-star-review-on-airbnb/

Fok, R. (2020, May 21). *300 days of hosting on Airbnb.* Medium. https://reneefok.medium.com/300-days-of-hosting-on-airbnb-adb48f38b0a9

A full guide to listing your vacation rentals on Vrbo. (2020, November 30). IGMS. https://www.igms.com/vrbo-listing/

Griffiths, C. (2020, February 18). *How to conduct an Airbnb market analysis.* Lifty Life. https://www.liftylife.ca/airbnb-market-analysis/

Griffiths, K. (2019, October 10). *How to rank #1 on Airbnb—the best Airbnb SEO advice.* Lifty Life. https://www.liftylife.ca/how-to-rank-on-airbnb/

He, S., & Svetec, J. (2022, March 17). *Airbnb for Dummies: Baseline pricing for your Airbnb.* John Wiley & Sons. https://www.dummies.com/article/home-auto-hobbies/travel/baseline-pricing-for-your-airbnb-271329/

How picture-perfect Airbnb photos increased bookings by $2,521. (2021, April 29). Rankbreeze. https://rankbreeze.com/airbnb-pictures/

How to ask Airbnb guests for 5 stars. (n.d.). Hostaway. https://www.hostaway.com/how-to-ask-airbnb-guests-for-5-stars/

How to automate my Airbnb in 2021—5 easy tips. (n.d.). Hostaway. https://www.hostaway.com/how-to-automate-my-airbnb-in-2021-5-easy-tips/

How to find the best Airbnb pricing strategy. (2020, October 30). Hosty. https://www.hostyapp.com/how-to-find-the-best-airbnb-pricing-strategy/#:~:text=If%20you%20offer%20less%20value

How to identify your target Airbnb guest—pro tips. (2020, July 27). LearnBNB. https://learnbnb.com/target-rental-audience-on-airbnb/

How to screen Airbnb guest in three simple stages? (2021, March 19). Hosty. https://www.hostyapp.com/how-to-screen-airbnb-guest/

How to start an Airbnb business? (n.d.). Hostaway. https://www.hostaway.com/how-to-start-an-airbnb-business/

How to take great Airbnb photos: An essential guide for success. (2020, November 24). IGMS. https://www.igms.com/airbnb-photos/#How_to_Take_the_Best_Airbnb_Photos_9_Helpful_Hints

Hrovat, J. (2021, May 24). *Our proprietary 3 step pricing formula to earn an additional $1,250 every month.* Beyond BNB. https://www.beyondbnb.io/post/3-step-pricing-formula

The inside story behind the unlikely rise of Airbnb. (2017, April 26). Knowledge at Wharton. https://knowledge.wharton.upenn.edu/article/the-inside-story-behind-the-unlikely-rise-of-airbnb/

Is Airbnb safe, reliable, and legal? (2022, March 11). TechBoomers. https://techboomers.com/t/is-airbnb-safe

Kelsey, K. (2019, September 15). *Finding a profitable Airbnb property.* AirHost Academy. https://airhostacademy.com/finding-airbnb-property/

Kidd, S. (2022, April 19). *Ultimate Airbnb cleaning checklist + free template.* TurnoverBnB. https://turnoverbnb.com/airbnb-cleaning-checklist/

Kovachevska, M. (2022, March 18). *28 amazing Airbnb statistics you should know before booking.* CapitalCounselor. https://capitalcounselor.com/airbnb-statistics/

Krones, T. (2020, July 3). *How to automate your Airbnb rental & increase efficiency.* Host Tools. https://hosttools.com/blog/short-term-rental-automation/automating-airbnb-rental/

Krones, T. (2020, August 7). *Airbnb house rules template: 15 examples of essential house rules for every listing.* Host Tools. https://hosttools.com/blog/short-term-rental-tips/airbnb-house-rules/

Krones, T. (2020, November 13). *The best Airbnb pricing tools for small hosts in 2021.* Host Tools. https://hosttools.com/blog/short-term-rental-tools/best-airbnb-pricing-tool/

Krones, T. (2021, March 2). *Is Airbnb profitable for hosts? Everything you need to know.* Host Tools. https://hosttools.com/blog/airbnb-rentals/is-airbnb-profitable-for-hosts/

Krones, T. (2021, July 5). *Airbnb photography: 8 tips to taking the perfect Airbnb photos.* Host Tools. https://hosttools.com/blog/short-term-rental-tips/airbnb-photography-guide/?swcfpc=1

Kutcher, J. (2020, January 31). *10 tips for running a successful Airbnb.* Jenna Kutcher Blog. https://jennakutcherblog.com/10-tips-for-running-a-successful-airbnb/

Lake, R. (2021, August 31). *Does your homeowner's insurance cover Airbnb?* Investopedia. https://www.investopedia.com/articles/insurance/120816/does-your-homeowners-insurance-cover-airbnb.asp

Lang, L. (2018, January 25). *23 things to do to prepare your home for Airbnb guests.* The SpareFoot Blog. https://www.sparefoot.com/self-storage/blog/20259-23-things-to-do-to-prepare-your-home-for-airbnb-guests/

Lara, J. (2021, April 24). *How to start an Airbnb. Ask yourself these 8 questions first.* Short Term Sage. https://shorttermsage.com/how-to-start-an-airbnb-business/

Lauzon, A. (2022, March 3). *Is Airbnb profitable in 2022?* Mashvisor Real Estate Blog. https://www.mashvisor.com/blog/is-airbnb-profitable/

Leonhardt, M. (2019, July 8). *82% of people think Airbnb-ing their home is a good money-making strategy—here's what you need to know.* CNBC. https://www.cnbc.com/2019/07/03/is-running-an-airbnb-profitable-heres-what-you-need-to-know.html

Manage multiple channels at scale. (n.d.) Guesty. https://www.guesty.com/features/channel-manager/#:~:text=A%20channel%20manager%20gives%20yous. (n.d.). Guesty.

Must-have Airbnb tools & apps. (n.d.). Hostaway. https://www.hostaway.com/must-have-airbnb-tools-and-apps/

Nix, D. (n.d.). *The ultimate insurance guide for Airbnb hosts.* Steadily. https://www.steadily.com/blog/airbnb-insurance-guide

O'Connell, C. (2022, June 9). *Best Airbnb descriptions to drive more bookings.* Guesthook. https://guesthook.com/best-airbnb-descriptions/

Plus vs Luxe: Comparing different types of Airbnb rentals. (2019, November 7). GuestReady. https://www.guestready.com/blog/airbnb-rentals-overview/

Protect your investment: Airbnb safety tips for hosts. (2018, November 7). Hosty. https://www.hostyapp.com/protect-investment-airbnb-safety-tips-hosts/

Responsible hosting in the United States. (n.d.). Airbnb. https://www.airbnb.ca/help/article/1376/responsible-hosting-in-the-united-states?locale=en&_set_bev_on_new_domain=1655368744_ZDBhODY1ZGUyODc0

Russell, T. (2019, November 12). *15 tips on how to automate your Airbnb property.* Short Rental Pro. https://www.shortrentalpro.com/15-tips-on-how-to-automate-your-airbnb-property/

Safety tips for hosts of places to stay. (n.d.). Airbnb. https://www.airbnb.ca/help/article/231/safety-tips-for-hosts-of-places-to-stay

Screening Airbnb guests. (n.d.). Renting Your Place. http://rentingyourplace.com/airbnb-101/airbnb_property_management/screening-guests/

7 tips for staying safe and secure as an Airbnb host. (2018, March 16). Fing. https://www.fing.com/news/7-tips-to-staying-safe-and-secure-as-an-airbnb-host

A step-by-step guide on how to list on Airbnb. (2018, November 26). Guesty. https://www.guesty.com/blog/step-by-step-guide-how-to-list-on-airbnb/

Suknanan, J. (2021, March 18). *Airbnb hosts shared 19 of their best tips for getting a five-star rating*. BuzzFeed. https://www.buzzfeed.com/jasminsuknanan/airbnb-five-star-review-hosting-tips

10 things to consider before hosting on Airbnb. (2020, July 27). LearnBNB. https://learnbnb.com/10-things-to-consider-before-hosting-on-airbnb/

3 biggest Airbnb myths busted. (2018, June 3). HelpHost. https://www.helphost.com/chicagoairbnbblog/3-biggest-airbnb-myths-busted

Tips on how to write Airbnb house rules. (2020, July 2). MasterHost. https://masterhost.ca/airbnb-house-rules/

Top 12 Airbnb competitors and alternatives for hosts. (2020, July 3). iGMS. https://www.igms.com/airbnb-competitors/

289+ great Airbnb host review examples (July 2022 update). (2022, July). Eat, Sleep, Wander. https://eatsleepwander.com/host-review-example/

Types of places to stay. (n.d.). Airbnb. https://www.airbnb.ca/help/article/5/types-of-places-to-stay#section-heading-0-0

The ultimate Airbnb host checklist: Everything you need to host successfully. (2022, August 17). Floorspace. https://www.getfloorspace.com/airbnb-host-checklist/

An ultimate guide to Airbnb automation. (2021, July 18). Zeevou. https://zeevou.com/blog/an-ultimate-guide-on-how-to-automate-airbnb-management/

Wade, T. (2018, September 27). *Airbnb home insurance—what you need to know*. Ratehub. https://www.ratehub.ca/blog/airbnb-home-insurance-what-you-need-to-know/

What are Airbnb's policies? (n.d.). Guesty. https://www.guesty.com/vacation-rental-guide/airbnb-policies/

What is a channel manager and why it's important. (n.d.). Hostaway. https://www.hostaway.com/what-is-a-vacation-rental-channel-manager/

What is Airbnb and how does it work? (n.d.). Airbnb. https://www.airbnb.ca/help/article/2503/what-is-airbnb-and-how-does-it-work

What regulations apply to my city? (n.d.). Airbnb. https://www.airbnb.ca/help/article/961/what-regulations-apply-to-my-city?locale=en&_set_bev_on_new_domain=1655368744_ZDBhODY1ZGUyODc0

When (not) to use Instant Book on Airbnb. (2018, March 1). GuestReady's Airbnb Hosting Blog. https://www.guestready.com/blog/airbnb-instant-book/

Why professional photography is important for Airbnb bookings. (n.d.). MadeComfy. https://www.blog.madecomfy.com.au/blog/professional-photography-a-deciding-factor-in-booking-short-term-stays

Yes, you need insurance to be an Airbnb host. (n.d.). Six Figures Under. https://www.sixfiguresunder.com/insurance-to-be-an-airbnb-host/

Zaidi, T. (2022, March 24). *Airbnb's cancellation and refund policy (flexible, moderate, strict).* TRVLGUIDES. https://trvlguides.com/articles/airbnb-cancellation-refund-policy

Zaqout, K. (2017, November 30). *What's the best property type for short-term rentals?* Mashvisor Real Estate Blog. https://www.mashvisor.com/blog/airbnb-apartment-vs-airbnb-house/

Zaragoza, R. (2021, November 26). *Conducting accurate Airbnb rental market analysis in 7 steps.* Mashvisor Real Estate Blog. https://www.mashvisor.com/blog/airbnb-rental-market/

IMAGE REFERENCES

Bezanger, J. (2021, June 5) [Image]. Unsplash. https://unsplash.com/photos/9k_gCYLoH2g

Carstens-Peter, J. (2017, Feb 6) *If you feel the desire to write a book, what would it be about?* [Image]. Unsplash. *https://unsplash.com/photos/npxXWgQ33ZQ*

Cottonbro. (2020, July 11) *Group of friend inside a dormitory.* [Image]. Pexels. https://www.pexels.com/photo/group-of-friend-inside-a-dormitory-5158945/

Dancre, R. (2020, October 27) *People signing documents for a wedding.* [Image]. Unsplash. https://unsplash.com/photos/doplSDELX7E

Glenn, K. (2018, March 18) [Image]. Unsplash. https://unsplash.com/photos/xY4r7y-Cllo

Gudakov, Z. (2021, August 10) *Red house.* [Image]. Unsplash. https://unsplash.com/photos/faBWQt9i7dg

Hendry, A. J. (2019, February 2) [Image]. Unsplash. https://unsplash.com/photos/KNt4zd8HPb0

Karpovich, V. (2020, March 21) *Woman working at home using laptop.* [Image]. Pexels. https://www.pexels.com/photo/woman-working-at-home-using-laptop-4050291/

Kayden, R. (2021, August 5) [Image]. Unsplash. https://unsplash.com/photos/FARBiTC4Bm0

Lach, R. (2021, December 20) *Bottles of cleaning products standing on metal shelf.* [Image]. Pexels. https://www.pexels.com/photo/bottles-of-cleaning-products-standing-on-metal-shelf-10558189/

Mallorca, T. (2019, June 14) [Image]. Unsplash. https://unsplash.com/photos/NpTbVOkkom8

Nickson, R. (2020, January 10) *The Juniper Room, Whisper Rock Ranch, Joshua Tree, California.* [Image]. Unsplash. https://unsplash.com/photos/emqnSQwQQDo

Perkins, P. (2017, August 13) *Airbnb.* [Image]. Unsplash. https://unsplash.com/photos/3wylDrjxH-E

Picjumbo. (2016, October 24). *Person holding blue ballpoint pen writing in notebook.* [Image]. Pexels. https://www.pexels.com/photo/person-holding-blue-ballpoint-pen-writing-in-notebook-210661/

Pixabay. (2014, February 13) *Security logo.* [Image]. Pexels. https://www.pexels.com/photo/security-logo-60504/

Schaffner, A. (2021, June 1) *Taking some pictures with my youngest daughter.* [Image]. Unsplash. https://unsplash.com/photos/n5OqZ-sDbSI

Scholz, S. (2019, May 16) *Nuki smart lock.* [Image]. Unsplash. https://unsplash.com/photos/IJkSskfEqrM

Spacejoy. (2021, April 12) [Image]. Unsplash. https://unsplash.com/photos/vOa-PSimwg4

Tankilevitch, P. (2020, May 1) *A person cleaning the table with cleaning cloth.* [Image]. Pexels. https://www.pexels.com/photo/a-person-cleaning-the-table-with-cleaning-cloth-4440608/

Terry Magallanes. (2019, February 7). *Four Brown Wooden Chairs.* [Image]. Pexels. https://www.pexels.com/photo/four-brown-wooden-chairs-2635038/

NOTES

1. AIRBNB BASICS

1. *Airbnb Statistics iPropertyManagement, 2022*
2. *The inside story behind the unlikely rise of Airbnb.* (2017, April 26)

3. THE TRUTH ABOUT AIRBNB HOSTING—MYTH VS. REALITY

1. *2022 Airbnb statistics: Usage, demographics, and revenue growth*
2. *Airbnb statistics.* (2022, May 4). iPropertyManagement.

4. 9 SIGNS STARTING AN AIRBNB BUSINESS IS RIGHT FOR YOU

1. *Airbnb Statistics iPropertyManagement, 2022*

6. HOW TO ANALYZE THE PLAYING FIELD

1. *2022 Airbnb statistics: Usage, demographics, and revenue growth*

7. PROS AND CONS OF RENTING OUT DIFFERENT PROPERTY TYPES

1. (2022, May 11). *Frank Lloyd Wright homes, farm stays, glamping sites—Airbnb's new search categories feature these cool listings*

10. SAFETY TIPS FOR HOSTS

1. 2021, June 15). *Airbnb is spending millions of dollars to make nightmares go away.* Bloomberg

11. THE ULTIMATE CHECKLIST FOR ITEMS TO BUY FOR YOUR PROPERTY

1. (2022, March 18). *28 amazing Airbnb statistics you should know before booking.* CapitalCounselor

14. LEGAL REGULATIONS TO CONSIDER

1. (2022, March 18). *28 amazing Airbnb statistics you should know before booking.* CapitalCounselor

17. THE PRICE IS RIGHT—STRATEGIES FOR MAXIMIZING PROFITS AND INCOME

1. *Average Airbnb prices by city: How much should you charge for your Airbnb? [2022]* (2022, May 2).

27. WHEN AND HOW TO USE AUTOMATION FOR YOUR AIRBNB RENTAL

1. *Airbnb Automation: 7 Ways To Put Your Business on Autopilot.* (2021, June 01

HOW TO UNLEASH YOUR AIRBNB'S FULL POTENTIAL

THE COMPLETE STEP-BY-STEP GUIDE TO MAXIMIZING BOOKINGS, RENTAL INCOME, SETTING UP AUTOMATION AND OPTIMIZATIONS FOR YOUR SHORT-TERM RENTAL BUSINESS

INTRODUCTION

There are currently over 6 million Airbnb listings on the platform (Woodward, 2022). It is crazy to think that there are so many. This means there is a lot of competition when it comes to short-term rentals. The positive side is that business is booming, and it is a good time to be on the market. The downside is that it is very competitive, and you need to be innovative if you want to stand out from the crowd. You need to prove why your Airbnb is better than any of its competitors. This way, you can maximize your booking potential and make sure that your calendar is always full.

You may be someone who is just starting out on Airbnb, or perhaps you have been a host for quite some time. Either way, there are definitely some challenges when it comes to ensuring you meet your Airbnb's potential. Perhaps there are some seasons in the year where bookings are not as good as you would like them to be. You might've noticed a dip in your bookings, or perhaps you struggled to get your Airbnb off the ground in the first place. You may be part of a completely different group of people who have decided to increase their capacity when it comes to Airbnb and are struggling to balance everything. All of these are valid struggles. The good news is that there are solutions to all of them.

In my personal experience, all it takes is a few tools to help take your Airbnb business to the next level. I have managed to grow my short-term rental business to the point where I am making a sizable income. I started my journey small, like most of us, and by implementing the tips and tricks I will share in this book, I have increased my capacity and productivity. On top of that, I am able to deliver top-quality service to all of my guests, and I've made the entire process a lot easier for myself as well. This is what I would like to share with you—it is not something that is only possible for a few people. Every person who is in the short-term rental industry is able to maximize their growth and income.

In the world of short-term rentals, there can be a lot of confusing information. It can seem like there are always new tools and technologies that come out. This makes it difficult to decide which ones are actually going to be beneficial for you. In this book, we will go through all things Airbnb and make sure that you can choose the right avenues to increase your income and profitability. You can also make your life much easier by using technology to automate many areas of your Airbnb rental business.

This is a very exciting time in the Airbnb industry. There is a lot of growth, and if you use the right tools, you'll be able to beat the competition and make your Airbnb stand out from the rest. Eventually, you'll grow your business to the point where you have multiple vacation rentals booked out like crazy. Some strategies are incredibly simple and don't take a lot of work to implement, while others do take a bit of elbow grease to get moving. However, all of them are valuable and can add something to your Airbnb business. All you need is to know the right information so you can get moving. There has never been a better time to start, so we are going to dive right in.

1

UNDERSTANDING THE MARKET

Building a successful Airbnb business hinges on understanding the market. Finding out what your guests really want means you can cater to their needs and ensure they leave happy with their stay. Understanding the market allows you to predict their wants and needs, so you are always one step ahead. This leads you to outperform your competitors, setting you apart from the pack.

CONDUCTING MARKET RESEARCH

Market research is the backbone of understanding the market. It is like studying before the big exam. You need to take steps to find out the relevant information. After doing this research, you will have a much better understanding, so you can make informed decisions on your pricing, listing, and any other important aspects of running your Airbnb.

Find Out More about Your Competition

Running an Airbnb is a competitive business. Hundreds of Airbnbs near yours could offer similar benefits to guests. This means you are competing for the same pool of potential guests. Knowing as much as you can about the competition puts you in a better position to beat them. As they say, knowledge is power.

When you are looking for your direct competitors, those will be the ones in the area where your property is located. Look at the Airbnb platform to get an idea of the properties in your area. See what they are offering to guests and how they advertise themselves. You may notice a few commonalities between them, and this gives you an indication of the trends. The properties with the highest ratings and the most bookings will be the ones that are doing something right, so pay special attention to those Airbnbs. It is also a good idea to take note of their unique selling points and anything extra they offer guests.

To help keep track of all this information, you can create a spreadsheet. Fill in all the information so it is easy to read. You will be able to organize it so you can see your direct competition and the strategies that are bringing in the most money.

Compare the Pricing Models

Pricing is one of the most important things to consider when you run an Airbnb. Even if you have the most amazing property in the world, nobody is going to book with you if it is way overpriced. You will also end up losing out on a large amount of profit if you underprice your property. Understanding the pricing of the Airbnb competitors in the area will give you insight into what you can charge. When comparing, make sure you are only comparing your prices to those of similar properties. It isn't going to work if you try to match prices for your one-bedroom apartment with a four-bedroom house. Look for direct competitors and develop your pricing model from there.

Look at the Reviews

The reviews of your competitors' Airbnbs give you a ton of information. You will find out what guests liked and didn't like. There is a chance that those same people would book an Airbnb in the same area, and if you can provide something that your competitors could not, you can attract new guests. For example, you might notice a few guests were upset by the lack of clean towels and sheets in one of your competitor's Airbnbs. You can make sure you have enough of these items in an easy-to-find closet. It would also be a good idea to highlight this in your listing so guests know they will not face this problem if they book with you.

Understand Your Guests

Knowing who your guests are goes a long way when it comes to understanding their needs. It can be tempting to try to cater to a wide variety of guests, but the problem with doing this is that you risk missing the mark for *all* guests. It is very difficult to cater to a family with small kids the same way you would to a group of friends in their early 20s looking for a good time. You will need to make compromises, and it is risky. Focusing on one type of guest will help you zero in on what you should be providing them, and you will end up with happier customers.

Your property's location, size, and amenities will have an impact on the type of guests you attract. Make sure you consider all of this before you decide on your target market. Any reviews or feedback you receive needs to be looked into. Your guests are a wealth of information. Try not to get upset or defensive if you do get a negative review. Rather, look into it and let the guest know you will fix it for their next stay.

This is especially important if the review is on public platforms. People will look at how you handled the feedback before booking with you. If you have addressed the concern, then this should not impact your bookings, and it will show that you are really concerned about meeting your guests' needs.

RECOGNIZING PEAK SEASONS AND EVENTS

Understanding your area's peak seasons and popular events helps you plan and set your prices accordingly. When accommodation is in demand, you have the opportunity to raise your prices since more people want to book. In slow seasons, you can reduce your prices to encourage people looking for a deal to book your Airbnb. Different areas will have different peak seasons. If you have a beach bungalow, summer is going to be when people want to book with you to enjoy the beach. A mountain cabin might have its peak season in winter because it's cozy, and the snow will be a fun experience for families.

Peak seasons can shift from time to time. This is why it is important to keep an eye out for what is happening in the travel world. After all the lockdowns from the pandemic a few years ago, there has been an uptick in shoulder-season travel (the period of time between a region's peak season and offseason). This means the traditional peak seasons have shifted slightly to include the few weeks before and after them. We don't know how long this trend is going to last, and there could be even more shifts in peak seasons in the future. It is a good idea to do your research on this each year so you are fully prepared.

An event can be anything that brings people to the area. There may be festivals, conferences, or showcases. It is important to stay connected with the community where your Airbnb is located, even if that is not where you live. Connecting with community groups in the area is a great way to know what is going on. When there is an event that will draw a crowd, you can raise the prices to match the demand and maximize profit.

At points in time when demand is low, you have to be a bit more aggressive when it comes to your marketing strategies. Making a few changes to your listing and requirements can make a huge difference. If you offer a discount, it is important to make this known. You can change the title of your listing to include the word "discount." This will make people more aware of the price drop. You can also reduce the minimum night requirement and change your cancellation policy to be more flexible. These small changes remove barriers and make it easier to draw people in when it's normally more difficult.

CONNECTION WITH LOCAL TOURISM OPERATORS AND BUSINESSES

Running an Airbnb is a great way to improve the community if you do it right. You are bringing more people into the area, which means you can bring in new business. Many small businesses miss out when it comes to tourism because visitors are not aware of them. As an Airbnb host, you have a unique opportunity to bring attention to these small businesses and create a stronger community.

When people go to a new city or area, they rely on the recommendations of their Airbnb host since they do not have any previous knowledge of the place. You can establish yourself as a trustworthy place by making good recommendations that are not as common and well-known. This will add to your guests' experience, and the small business owners will benefit as well.

A great way to do this is to incorporate some local treats and flavors into a welcome box for your guests. You can connect with local businesses and vendors to see if they would like to collaborate with you to get some exposure. This means you could get a discount on the items in your welcome box or get them completely free if the business owners agree. You may be able to access discounts for your guests. Perhaps free coffee or drinks with a meal are offered at certain restaurants. Another option is asking for "buy one, get one free" cards from business owners.

Incorporating the local vibe into your guests' packages is a great way to create an entire experience for them. This can be an optional add-on for them to purchase when they make the booking. Perhaps have an option for local fresh flowers to be added to the room or a local meal to be delivered to them on the day of arrival.

The options are truly endless when it comes to incorporating local businesses into your business. You get the added benefit of word of mouth. Anyone who shops at a local business you have partnered with will hear about you. This could drum up more bookings for you and make you more known among locals and those living in neighboring towns.

2

STRATEGIC PRICING 101

You have an amazing Airbnb in a wonderful location, but it isn't making as much money as you thought. Ever wonder why that is? Your pricing strategy could be the culprit. Sometimes, it's not about the physical Airbnb but about other factors, such as price. Price plays a huge role in whether people want to book with you. It also influences whether you make the most profit from your Airbnb.

THE BASICS OF DYNAMIC AND STATIC PRICING

There are two main strategies when it comes to pricing: dynamic and static pricing. When you are thinking of a pricing strategy, these are typically the two that would be suggested that you would think of. One tool that can be used is called Airbnb Smart Pricing. This tool will adjust your pricing depending on many different factors. It helps you keep your rates competitive without having to change the prices manually all the time. Your pricing will be automatically updated depending on what is going on in the market. If there is more demand in your area, the price will automatically go up, and in seasons where the demand is lower, it brings the prices down. This gives you a better opportunity to get bookings based on what people are looking for and is more of a dynamic pricing strategy.

Before going any further, let's discuss dynamic and static pricing. Dynamic pricing is when the price of an Airbnb listing changes as time goes on. Sometimes, people are willing to pay more for an Airbnb, and there are others when they will be looking for cheaper deals. Let's say you have a beach bungalow as your Airbnb. People will probably want to book with you in the summer when they can enjoy the beach and the sunshine. Your peak times will be during the summer holidays and weekends. Your off-peak times will be in the winter and during the week. Understandably, people are not as drawn to the beach in the colder months as in the summer months. You can charge more in the summer because people want to go on vacation. They are willing to pay more, and places will quickly get booked. In the winter months, people won't be as likely to book, so in order to draw them in, the price will need to be lower. Changing the prices depending on demand is a dynamic pricing strategy.

There is a lot to consider regarding a dynamic pricing strategy. There are plenty of ways to do it, and it sometimes takes trial and error to figure out what is going to work for you in your specific area and market. Another way to incorporate dynamic pricing into your pricing strategy is to look at the dates you have available. The most popular date could be booked up, and you have a bunch of random dates here and there that are not getting booked. This is pretty common, and it might be a good idea to use a dynamic pricing strategy to draw in some potential guests. If you bring the price down for those specific days, people are more likely to want to book with you. You would end up beating out the competition, who are all vying for a very small number of guests. In a competitive market like this, it is going to work in your favor if you do your best to beat the competition with your low prices. Just remember that you don't want to put it so low that you aren't making any profit at all.

If you use a dynamic pricing strategy, you may want to consider a few tools. These will help you access the data needed to make better choices. Many of the tools can also change the prices based on what is happening in the market, which makes things easier for you. There are quite a few tools on the market, and they are constantly being updated. Keeping up-to-date on the development of the tools in this space will allow you to choose the ones that will benefit you most. A few to look into are Airbnb's Smart Pricing, AirDNA's Smart Rates, Beyond, PriceLabs, and Wheelhouse.

Then, we have a static pricing strategy, which just means the price stays the same. You will decide on a price that suits you and leave it for the duration of your Airbnb business listing. It is much easier to handle static pricing since you do not have to change it all the time. However, the problem with this is that you are potentially missing out on revenue because you're not using a pricing strategy that changes with the market. Your pricing might work in the summer months, but it would be too expensive for people to pay in the winter months. You are now losing out on all potential guests in the winter, so your property stands vacant for a longer period of time than it should.

You can use static pricing to your advantage if you also consider adding discounts for longer stays. It is usually more beneficial for your property to be booked for a longer period of time. If someone is simply booking for one day, it can get in the way of other people being able to book. For example, somebody could book for one Saturday, and this means that any potential weekend holiday-goers will not be able to book your property. It gets in the way of them potentially booking a Friday to a Sunday, which would bring in more money. Encouraging longer booking stays helps you maximize your profit, even with a static strategy. For example, you could keep your booking price at a higher rate and then start offering discounts with more days booked. I would start with your high rate for a one-night stay, which will probably discourage people from booking one night. Then offer a 10 percent discount if the person books for two nights and a 15 percent discount if they book for three. Now, you have created the opportunity for potential guests to think about whether they can book for longer, which would discourage one-night stays. This leaves your property open for longer bookings and increases your overall revenue.

GENERAL PRICING GUIDE

Before you decide whether to use a dynamic or static pricing model, you can use a general pricing system to help you set your prices.

This will help you get the most out of your pricing without having to constantly change it or put in as much active work. Using a general pricing guide is a good idea to get your base pricing right so you know what to charge, even if you are looking to implement more dynamic strategies.

The first thing you will need to do is start researching your competition in the local area. Almost every area already has Airbnbs. This means there is already a general price that people are willing to pay in order to stay there. You can take a look at your competition to find out how much they are charging and what they are offering. If you charge too much, you risk your competitors getting all the guests, but if you charge too little, you end up losing money. Remember to only compare your property to ones that are similar to yours so you can understand what price you should use and what your potential guests would be willing to pay.

To discover the general pricing in your area, you will need to jump into the shoes of a potential guest. Log into the Airbnb platform as a guest and then start searching for properties in your area. Put in the filters that are applicable to your Airbnb and see what shows up. The next thing you will do is click on the price range filter, which will show you the average price for the date range you selected. This filter only gives you the average price, which means that any excessively expensive or cheap outliers will impact the price you are seeing. You need to exclude these outliers since they skew the average and don't give you an accurate view of what people are willing to pay. All you have to do is move the minimum price up and the maximum price down so that you remove all the outliers, and it should give you a better idea of the average price people are willing to pay.

Also, look at the number of available listings for the criteria and filters you have placed. This will give you a good idea of how many rentals are offering the same thing as you and how big your competition is. It is a good idea to check both types of information for every single month of the year, as they can change. You can create a spreadsheet for yourself to note the average nightly price and the number of listings for each month. You can then set different prices for each month, taking advantage of the changes in season. For example, in months when fewer listings are available, you can increase your price by 10 to 20 percent, as there is less competition in the area.

PRICING STRATEGIES FOR DIFFERENT PROPERTY TYPES

It is so important to fully understand your property type before you choose a pricing strategy. This is because the type of property will play a direct role in how much people are willing to pay to stay there. Someone who is just looking for a room with a bathroom is going to pay a lot less than somebody who is looking for a fully furnished apartment. When looking at your competition, you have to take into account the types of properties they have, as well as the amenities they offer. You will need to identify your direct competition in order to price your properties correctly.

When you create a listing on Airbnb, you'll be asked for your arrangement type, and there are four basic types to choose from. These are an entire home, a hotel room, a private room, and a shared room. An entire home would be the most expensive of the arrangements, while a shared room would be a lot cheaper. However, with a shared room, if you do have an entire property, it means that you can have multiple guests who stay in one home. This could result in you ending up with more profit due to the way you are listing your property on Airbnb. However, it is important to note that each arrangement type targets a specific type of guest. That is why it is important to know who your guests are and what they need so you can cater to them directly.

Amenities are such an important part of creating a pricing strategy or a price base point. Some Airbnb hosts provide the bare necessities, and others go over and above to provide more amenities for the guests. A property that has amazing amenities will be able to charge more because it offers more. Some great examples of amenities that people are willing to pay more for include hot tubs, swimming pools, gaming rooms, or even fantastic views and easy access to things like the beach.

When you are trying to figure out how much you should charge for your property, you will need to use the filters so you can see the properties that offer similar amenities to yours. It is a good idea to do a deep dive into the pricing of all the properties in your area so you can get a better idea of what they offer and how you can be different. Adding an amenity that most properties do not have in your area can be a huge benefit because it makes you stand out from the rest of the properties. Not only that, but you can start charging slightly higher rates because you are adding more value to your guests.

Now that you have a solid understanding of the basics and the most fundamental aspects of Airbnb pricing, it is time for us to dive a little deeper. In the next chapter, we are going to explore more advanced pricing strategies. These are the tools the top Airbnb hosts use to optimize their income.

3

ADVANCED PRICING STRATEGIES

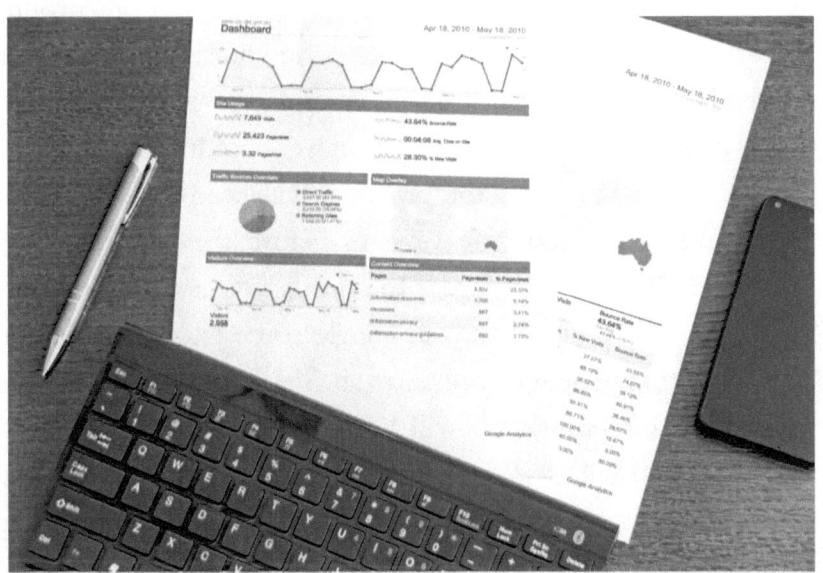

Not long ago, the keywords "Airbnb collapse" were trending on Twitter. It's usually not a good idea to get your information from social media, but it was interesting to see how many people jumped on the bandwagon to say that Airbnb was going down and the prices would need to start dropping. It is no secret that many Airbnb hosts feared this becoming a reality, but the truth is that much of this can be avoided by using the right pricing strategies. Like other businesses, Airbnb goes through highs and lows in terms of average revenue. Knowing how to preempt this and ensuring that your pricing strategy matches what is going on in the market will lead you to create a sustainable and long-lasting business. Not only that, but you will be able to create an Airbnb business that brings in the maximum amount of profit possible.

Before diving into the different scenarios for changing your Airbnb pricing strategy, let's talk about it as someone who is new to the Airbnb market. When you first start out on Airbnb, you are not going to have any reviews on your listing. Reviews are the lifeblood of an Airbnb. The more reviews you have, the more people trust you and the more bookings you'll get. Someone who is new to the platform will need to focus their energy on getting positive reviews before they can start to maximize their profit. In order to do this, you need to set your price quite a bit lower than your competitors. This is so you can start attracting people to your Airbnb. Since you cannot win on reviews at this point, you will have to win on price. It does mean that you will lose out on profit, but the truth is that you need to build a base before you even have a chance to make a sustainable and long-term profit.

After you have a good number of reviews, you can start to slowly increase the price of your listing. You don't want to keep the price low for too long. Otherwise, you will be missing out on potential profit. It is usually best to make it a gradual increase rather than slapping a doubled price tag on your Airbnb. Over the course of the next few months, you will slowly increase the price until you are happy with the amount that you are charging and are sure this will bring the maximum amount of profit for you. At this point, you should have a good number of reviews, which means that you have more credibility in the market.

STRATEGIES FOR WEEKDAYS AND WEEKENDS

Setting up different prices for weekends and weekdays is pretty crucial to maximizing your Airbnb profits. Most people go away on vacation on the weekend, and if your property is a vacation rental, this will be your most in-demand time. Also, people who want to stay in the Airbnb during the week usually do so for work and are not planning to relax or enjoy the accommodation. This means they are more likely to choose the cheapest option than the option that is going to offer them the most amenities.

Many Airbnbs change their price depending on the time of the week, so you can have a look at your competitors to see how they price. This will give you a good idea of what your base price should be, and then you can work from there—on weekends when there are events happening in your area, you can increase the price even more since accommodations in that area will be in demand.

STRATEGIES FOR ORPHAN DAYS

An orphan day or an orphan period is a day or a number of days that are in between bookings. If you have a minimum night's stay on your bookings, this can create an unbookable day in between. For example, someone could book from Monday to Wednesday, and another guest could book from Thursday to Sunday. This leaves Wednesday night open. If your minimum night's stay is set to two days, then nobody will be able to book out the Wednesday, and you will essentially be losing money due to this.

One of the easiest things to do for an orphan day is to reach out to either one of your guests and ask if they would be willing to book an extra night. You can offer a good discount for this night and not issue any additional fees, such as the cleaning fee. This way, it makes booking the extra night a lot more attractive, and you don't have to worry about having a random day open that is not bringing you any money. If one of the guests says no, then you can reach out to the other guest to see if they are willing to. You would be surprised at how many people are willing to extend their stay for a discount.

If neither of the guests wants to book the orphan night and your minimum night's stay is set to two nights, you will have to change it and allow a one-night stay for that date only. You may think a one-night stay is not worth it, especially if you have set a two-night minimum and are used to multi-night stays. However, you may be surprised at how much extra profit you can make by filling the gaps in your calendar.

Earlier, I mentioned how to filter search pricing on the Airbnb platform and find out what your competition is charging. You can use this method to search your area for similar listings on the date of the orphan night. When you search for the date that the orphan night occurred, you will most likely find that most of your competition is booked for this date. If that's the case and competition is low, you can increase your price for a single night, especially if it falls on a weekend. If the orphan night occurs in a slow season or in the week, many other listings will be available, and you should create a discount to attract a booking.

STRATEGIES BASED ON LEAD TIME

A booking lead time refers to the period between when the guest makes the reservation and the day they check in. For example, your guest could make a booking on November 5 and only check in on November 25. This means the booking lead time is twenty days. You can easily find out what your average booking lead time is by using Airbnb's professional tools option. While this information is definitely accurate, it would be better for you to track your bookings to find out when people are booking your Airbnb. Remember that average booking takes into consideration outliers, and it doesn't give you accurate information that you can actually work from.

The best thing you can do is create a small spreadsheet for yourself. In one column, you will put the different booking lead times in spaces of five days. Your first column will have zero to five days, your second six to ten, and so on. You will then fill in how many bookings you get within those lead times throughout the year. This way, you have an accurate idea of when people will commonly book and when they will not. This will give you better information so you can make more informed decisions about your pricing strategy.

If you notice fewer bookings as it gets closer to the day, you can start offering discounts to encourage people to book with you. The closer you get to the actual day, the more discounts you can offer until you reach the minimum booking price that you have set for yourself. However, the opposite could be true, where you get most of your bookings closer to the stay, and most of your guests do not book in advance. Having this information on hand means you are not going to panic when you are a few weeks away from a specific open date. You know that your guests typically book with shorter notice, and you can trust that information, so you don't have to bring down your prices or offer discounts, since you can still make a maximum amount of profit even with shorter booking lead times. You can adjust your prices based on the information you have gained from your booking lead time data.

Having a deep understanding of the market and your competitors will help you make better decisions when it comes to pricing. It is also important to know what is happening in your area, in terms of events and the booking patterns that your typical Airbnb guest displays. All of this allows you to have as much information as possible when it comes to setting your prices. Being able to set strategic prices can be the difference between being profitable and struggling.

4

TRANSITIONING AND DIVERSIFICATION

It is important to be flexible when it comes to your rental property business. There can be shifts and changes in the market that will render your current strategy ineffective. When this happens, many property investors get disheartened and sell up. Rather than looking at these situations as negatives, look at them as an opportunity to shift into something different. You will be able to maximize your profits, which will lead you to becoming more successful. A little bit of flexibility can lead to a much more stable property business year-round.

SHIFTING FROM SHORT-TERM RENTALS (STR) TO MID-TERM RENTALS (MTR)

I have personally found success using this strategy. A few years ago, after a busy summer season, I noticed that my bookings started to slow down. This was common for most hosts in my area. Weekend bookings remained strong, but fewer bookings came in during the week. Ultimately, prices started to decrease as most hosts competed for the same type of guest who stayed from Friday to Sunday.

This prompted me to start renting out my properties weekly or monthly to get through the slow season. I was happy to reduce my rate to attract longer-stay bookings. The idea of having a nearly 100 percent occupancy rate with fewer turnovers sounded good. I knew that construction had begun on a new Correctional Center that, when completed, could hold 1700 inmates. This project lasted several years. The prison was located in the middle of nowhere, and the nearest town with motels, shops, and pubs was about a twenty-minute drive away —exactly where my accommodation was situated.

There were some workers who moved to the area and rented permanent, unfurnished houses, but many companies also came for shorter periods to work on the construction site. Their workers had to stay in motels, which was costly. Airbnb listings in the area were not an option, as most hosts' calendars were already booked out for future weekends, making a month-long stay impossible in those Airbnbs.

One day, I drove to the prison's construction site, and the plan was to stick business cards on all car windshields, advertising my houses as fully furnished mid-term rentals. Unfortunately, the car park was gated, and security didn't allow me onto the construction site. Determined, I spent the next six hours parked in my car outside the construction entrance, taking note of all trucks and vans that entered or exited the site. Most of these vehicles had advertisements or company logos, so I collected their names and phone numbers. I called each one and inquired if they needed furnished mid-term accommodation. And you know what? It worked!

I managed to secure a group of temporary workers from out of town. They were initially staying in a motel, paying premium rates. We agreed on a minimum stay of six weeks with one week's notice before moving out. This group ended up staying for three months. As they left, they passed my number on to the next group of workers, who also booked with me for several weeks. This cycle continued, and those six hours spent in my car at the construction site turned out to be the best time investment for finding new guests. I accommodated carpenters, concreters, painters, electricians, plumbers, and fitters, all working on the same construction site.

Opportunities to increase business for your Airbnb are everywhere if you are willing to think outside the box. I had four solid years of mid-term bookings that brought in a steady income in the slow seasons, so those six hours in my car were totally worth it. Mid-term rentals are simply rentals that are longer than traditional short-term rentals. It bridges a gap and attracts a completely different type of guest. Many hosts do not even think of this as an option, and that means you will be one of the few who use this strategy. You will probably attract more guests and don't have to worry about not making an income in the slow periods.

Filling the Calendar with Monthly Bookings

After hearing my story, you might be thinking that shifting your strategy is a great idea—or maybe you need a little more convincing. The mid- to long-term market is increasing, and there is a definite need for more of these accommodations. The way people travel and live is changing, and this means people need places to stay on a mid-term basis. There is a rise in people who travel for work, are digital nomads, and are remote workers. These people want a place to stay so they can explore the area and don't have to worry about furnishing an apartment or staying in a hotel for a long time. Renting out your Airbnb on a long-term basis is the answer to this.

There are tons of tangible benefits that you can access when you change your strategy. One of the biggest risks associated with a short-term rental is the low turnover rate. This means it may take weeks or months before you are able to get another guest into your rental. In this case, you will have lost revenue because your property is standing empty. If you know there is a slow season coming up, it is the perfect time to start thinking about a mid-term strategy. This way, you don't have to lose out on revenue. You have the freedom to change the rates as demand increases and decreases to maximize your profit. This is not something that can be done with a long-term rental. With a mid-term rental, you get the flexibility of a short-term rental and the stability of a long-term one.

Another benefit is that it is simply easier to manage. You don't need to turn over the property every weekend. Since it is a longer stay, they will likely handle everything for themselves, and you just have to be on call in case of emergencies. You also don't have to replace items that have been used up because the guest will do their own grocery and toiletry shopping. This helps you save both time and money.

You will have peace of mind knowing that your property is bringing in money, but you don't have to do as much work. When the peak seasons roll around again, you can switch your strategy back to a short-term one so you can get the best of both worlds. Overall, you will increase your profits throughout the year and meet the needs of various types of guests.

When moving into a mid- or long-term strategy, the needs of the guests do change. Many short-term guests look for novelty and something different because they are on vacation. This is why you can attract them with themes, activities, and novelty products. However, it is not the same for mid-term and long-term guests. They are after more practicality since they are going to be calling this place home for a few weeks. You can highlight your property's more practical elements when marketing it to a new group of people. For example, you don't have to mention a welcome box or additional amenities like board games and other fun items. Rather, focus on bringing attention to Wi-Fi, a desk or office space, a quiet neighborhood, storage space, and other things that would be more attractive to someone who may be working from the location or in need of some rest after a long day at work.

INCREASING OCCUPANCY

Now that you have decided mid-term rentals are the way to go for the slower seasons, it is time to think about how you are going to increase your occupancy rates. These strategies can work with either short- or mid-term rentals; you just have to target the right audience. If you remain fluid with your approach, you will have a better chance of increasing your occupancy.

Work on Your Listing

Your listing is the most important part of attracting guests to your property. It is the first impression they get, and it will help them understand if your property is a good fit or not. Bookings are won and lost with a listing. You will need to make sure it is consistently updated and that you have all the relevant details in it. Since you are renting it out using different strategies, you should highlight when mid-term rentals are available so people are prepared for this.

In the peak seasons, your rental will target vacationers. This means your strategy will be focused on making the experience unique and enjoyable. Highlighting why potential guests should book with you is essential. There is more competition when it comes to short-term rentals, so you really need to sell it. Make it engaging and draw people in.

When you switch over to long- or mid-term rentals, people look for something different. They look for convenience and comfort. They don't want an overbearing landlord checking on them all the time and usually prefer to be left to their own devices. They will be bringing their own food and personal care items, so you will not have to worry about that. Instead, highlight what makes your property comfortable and feel like home. For example, if you have an extremely comfortable couch, you can highlight this and let them know there is nothing better than sinking into your plush sofa after a long day's work. Think about what you would want in your home away from home, and that should give you a good indication of what you should be highlighting.

Offer Discounts

Everybody loves a discount. If you offer one, you will get more people interested in your property. When moving to a mid-term strategy, you can highlight the discount guests will get if they book for a longer period of time. This will reel them in. Look at other discounts you can offer at specific times of the year, or even combine experiences with your booking. If you work with local vendors, you can get discounts for your guests for meals and activities. All of this is a huge draw.

Use Social Media

Social media is a great way to market your property. Many people just focus on the Airbnb platform, but this is a mistake. Even though you are hosting your listing on the platform, you should still market using whatever is available to you.

There is a large group of people who do not use Airbnb to find their rentals. This means you are missing out on this market. Using social media allows you to connect with them and show them what you're offering. You also have the benefit of short-form marketing, where you can make a post highlighting one aspect of your property at a time. It makes it easier for people to digest.

In today's world, people always go to social media to do research. Places with a social media presence are a lot more reputable and of better quality. This is why having this aspect of your property business really does help. It does take work, and you must be consistent with your posts to ensure you are getting the most out of social media. One of the best things you can do is plan your posts for the month. That way, you have everything ready to go. You can create and save drafts and only post them when you are ready. Set a reminder on your phone to post at specific times and days so you don't forget. All you have to do is click "post," and it will go live. It makes posting on social media a lot more manageable.

You will also need to engage with people in the comments and if they send you private messages. This boosts your credibility, and communication is always key when you are working with social media. You would be surprised at how many people get their information from the comments section of a post.

Increasing Your Airbnb's Capacity

One of the reasons someone may want to book an Airbnb rather than a hotel room is because it is bigger and more flexible. One of the best things you can do to attract more guests is to increase the capacity. All you need to do for this is add more sleeping spaces. This is an easy and cheap way to get more bookings. There could be a family with small children that needs an extra space or two.

You don't need to add an extra room to your property in order to do this. It is a simple fix. Adding a sofa bed or a bunk bed does not take up any extra space, and you get more sleeping space out of the deal. You increase your guest pool and allow more people to find you. Your listing can sleep more people, so you can add this to the listing. If you had a four-sleeper, you now have a five- or six-sleeper and are appealing to more people.

ADDITIONAL REVENUE SOURCES

There is plenty you can do to increase your revenue when you are renting out your property. This is a business, so it is important to think like a business owner. This helps you get into the mindset of finding more ways to increase revenue. The more revenue you create, the more profit you have and the more you can do with it.

Send a Questionnaire upon Booking

It is a big win to find out what your guests actually want and need. If you can give them additional services, you can make them happier and earn some extra money as well. The questionnaire does not ask them about their experience but rather creates a better one for them. You will also have the option to upsell certain things to them.

Remember to be transparent with this questionnaire and put the additional prices on it. Not every guest will want the additional services, but some will. Some ideas for additional services are a full fridge stock, airport pickup and transfers, daily cleaning, and taxi or transportation services. You can also include things like asking for their favorite wine, food, or snack in their welcome box. What you offer and ask with this questionnaire will depend on your capacity.

Customized Check-In and Checkout Times

Many guests would like to check in or check out at a different time than what is regularly stated. It takes very little effort from you to offer early or late check-in or check-out. Most guests are happy to pay extra for this. It does give you less time to turn over the property to the next guest, so bear this in mind.

Tours

If you are a resident of this area and know it well, you can offer tours. Many guests love to tour the local area and learn more about it. You could also hire a tour guide or affiliate yourself with a tour company.

Events and Celebrations

There are a huge number of guests who book an Airbnb because they are celebrating something. You can offer specific services for these celebrations. Offering a custom cake for birthdays, graduations, and anniversaries is something many guests will want. Depending on the occasion, you could also offer a celebration basket that includes champagne, a special meal, snacks, flowers, and balloons. There are tons of ways to make this work. You can add the price to the list so they are aware of it. Since many guests will be looking for places to get these items for their celebrations, you would be making their lives a lot easier.

Partner with Businesses

There are probably tons of small businesses around your Airbnb. Partnering with them will help you offer your guests unique experiences, contribute to the economy of the area, and make you some extra money. Most guests will look to you for guidance on what they should do, see, and eat in the area. Offering a custom package in which you plan their trip and guide them to all the different spots in the area helps them and you. Many businesses will be happy to offer discounts to you and your guests. Just make sure to reach out to these businesses first so you can work out a deal.

By following these transition and diversification strategies, you can ensure consistent income. But do note that successful implementation relies on understanding your performance and the market, which brings us to the next topic: data analytics and metrics.

5

DATA ANALYTICS AND METRICS

According to *Analytics Comes of Age* (2018), 36 percent of companies indicated that data and analytics have changed the competition in their industry. Also stated was that 32 percent of companies have changed their long-term strategies based on what they have learned from data and analytics. There is so much that can be learned. It helps you improve your strategy and takes your business to the next level.

THE POWER OF DATA ANALYTICS

More information is always going to be better when you are making decisions and building strategies for your business. It allows you to know what is actually going on in the market so you can react appropriately. So much can change over the years that simply using the same strategy is not going to work in the long term. In this business, it is important to remain flexible throughout the process.

When you go in blind, you risk making mistakes. Using data and analytical tools means that you don't have to take that risk. You have the information in front of you, so your strategies can be based on facts and real-time data. You no longer have to use the trial-and-error approach because you can learn from what is already happening. It is like learning from other people's mistakes rather than making the same ones yourself. You know what is most effective and what is causing the most growth for others, and it will probably do the same for you.

You will find that you are far more confident with your decisions, which means you can make them a lot more quickly. When we are unsure, it takes us longer to actually get going. There is a lot of beating around the bush because we are not confident in our actions. With data, you will be more proactive and can make choices more quickly. Data will be available to you in real time so you can be more effective in your strategies and ensure they are implemented almost immediately.

Using these tools means that you can also monitor yourself and your own business. You will be able to quickly notice if there is something different with bookings or revenue. The sooner you are aware of problems, the faster you can fix them. This means you are better prepared and more aware.

There are so many tools on the market that you are spoiled for choice. You can do your own research to find one that suits you best. Just remember to look at reviews and check what they offer so you can compare them properly. Most of the good ones require you to pay a fee to use them, so you want to ensure you are paying for quality. AirDNA is one of the best tools and has been around for quite some time. It collects and provides short-term rental data for the host so they can make more informed decisions. It has access to data from over 10 million rentals, so the information you get will be well-analyzed and true. AllTheRooms and KeyData are also good options to look into.

DIFFERENT METRICS TO TRACK

Many different metrics can be tracked to help you make better decisions. A good program will have all or most of these available. Make sure to check what is offered before you buy or subscribe to data and analytics software so you can be sure you are getting what you need.

Revenue per Available Room (RevPAR)

This is an essential metric, and almost all hotels and rental properties will use it. It helps to fully understand the performance of the property at any given point. You can easily recognize any gains or losses. This metric allows you to see how well your pricing strategy is working for you. It also allows you to see your overall profitability. It is very easy to work this out. Here is the formula:

$$RevPAR = \text{Average Daily Rate (ADR)} \times \text{Occupancy Rate}$$

Let's say your rental is booked 60 percent of the time, and your average daily rate is $100. This means your RevPAR is $60. You can track this to make sure you aren't dipping too low. If the overall number increases, then you know you are doing something right.

Average Daily Rate (ADR)

We used ADR to work out the previous metric, so you are probably wondering about it. This metric shows you the average amount your guests are paying per day at your rental property. Since it is common to offer discounts and there may be one-time fees applicable for a multiday booking, the nightly rate is not always accurate. Here is the formula:

ADR = Total Revenue / Number of Booked Nights

You will be using the total revenue, which means if you charge a cleaning fee or any other fee, this will need to be included. This way, you get a more accurate idea of your ADR.

Occupancy Rate

An occupancy rate can be measured using a percentage or simply by stating the number of days booked in a year. The occupancy rates are important because they affect the revenue your Airbnb makes. The more bookings a property gets, the more money it will make. Working out the occupancy rate is simple. Here is the formula:

Occupancy rate = number of booked nights / total number of nights available to be booked x 100%

You will get a percentage amount, so you can see how much of your total available bookings has been taken. If it is less than 50 percent, you will need to work on increasing your bookings in some way.

Response Rate and Acceptance Rate

This is important to understand because if it is low, then you are likely not getting many bookings. Your response rate shows you how often you respond to guests within 24 hours of them reaching out. Clear communication is essential when you are running an Airbnb. Guests will be looking at multiple potential bookings; usually, the ones that respond first have a higher chance of being booked. Your acceptance rate refers to how often you accept or decline booking requests and reservations. There could be many reasons you decline a reservation, but it is not a good thing to do this for no reason. It actually reflects badly on you on the Airbnb site.

These two metrics are easily located on the platform. The acceptance rate can be found in the performance tab under "Basic Requirements." This will show you your acceptance rate for the past 365 days. Only formal booking requests count towards this, so any messages and inquiries will not count.

Cancellation and Rejection Rates

These affect how successful you are on the Airbnb platform. Airbnb only wants to suggest reliable hosts, and this means if you are rejecting and canceling too often, it will affect how often you show up in search results. If you cancel too often, your account could be suspended, which is definitely not something you want. You should not cancel more than three times a year; otherwise, suspension could be the result. You will be able to find this information under the performance tab on the platform. If guests cancel with you, then your cancellation rate will not be affected. It is best to aim for zero percent, as this means you are the most reliable.

Now that we've explored the world of data analytics and metrics, it's time to apply this knowledge to the core of your Airbnb business—your listing.

6

OPTIMIZING YOUR AIRBNB LISTING

An optimized listing is your ticket to more bookings. Think about it: The first thing your guests will see is your listing. It is the first impression. In the first few seconds, your guests will decide whether your Airbnb is an option or if they should keep scrolling. You need to make your listing as appealing as possible so you can attract as many guests as possible.

WHY A COMPLETED LISTING MATTERS

Let's say you are looking to buy a house. The first place you look is on a property listing site. As you are scrolling through, you notice one that meets most of your requirements and is in your price range. Jackpot! You click on the listing, and there are only two pictures, one from the sidewalk. On top of that, the description is just one sentence. Do you bother messaging the agent? Probably not. This listing is incomplete, and that is an immediate red flag. The person who posted it clearly does not care about what they put forward, and this means that their house is not likely to be well cared for. You immediately click out and continue scrolling.

This is the same thing people do when looking at the Airbnb platform. At the end of the day, perception matters. Even if your property is the best priced and meets all its requirements, if your listing is incomplete, any potential guests will not trust you. A complete and well-done listing shows that you care about what you put out into the world, and it shows guests what they can expect. You can have all the best marketing strategies in the world, but it isn't going to matter if your listings are horrible.

The more detailed your listing, the better. Not all guests will go through every detail, but there are some who will want to. The guests who just want the basics can skim through, but at least the information is there for them should they want it. Before your guests even click on your listing, they will have a look at the cover photos. These need to draw them in, so your property's selling points need to be showcased here. Make sure all photos are of good quality. You will put the most important ones first, and then you can add all the rest after. Many guests don't read the description, but they will all look through the photos. Even if you need to hire a professional photographer, it is worth it. In my first book, *How to Set Up and Run a Successful Airbnb Business*, I go into more detail about getting the perfect pictures for your listing.

Your description is the next thing your guests might go through. It needs to be around 175 words. This is short enough not to bore them, but it also gives them enough details. Highlight key points that actually matter and that they would care about. You can also speak to the type of guest you are looking to attract. For example, if you want families to book with you, you can highlight how kid-safe and family-friendly your property is.

If you already have an Airbnb set up on the platform and have reviews, make sure you take a look at them. They might indicate things that the guests really loved and areas you can improve on. If you have taken the feedback on board and added amenities, make sure to add this to your description. These are things that your guests want, so it is important to showcase that you do have them. If your guests suggest something that would make the experience better, make sure to listen to them and do your best to get it in the future. You will be able to add the new updates to the listing. Sometimes, the smallest things make the biggest difference.

IMPROVING TITLE, DESCRIPTION, AND AMENITIES

Taking the time to craft your listing is essential. Even though they say a picture is worth a thousand words, your words also matter. Ensure you have the right title and description because this gives your potential guests the information they need. The title is what will draw them in and allow you to show up in the right search results. If the title is not appealing, you will get very few clicks. Use words that make the guest want to click rather than simply explaining the basics. Let's say you have a small property in the forest. A great title would be: Cozy Forest Hideaway. It shows the guests exactly what they can expect, but it also draws them in and allows curiosity to take over.

Your title will lead into the description, so you will need to carry the same energy over. It is so easy to just list out information, but nobody is excited to read a list. Try to tell a story with your words. This is the best way to get your point across and engage the potential guest. Your photos will give the guest a good idea of what you offer, but you need to describe the things that make your property stand out from the rest. The basics will already be listed, so you don't have to indicate the number of rooms, bathrooms, and amenities. Use this space to tell your guests about the surroundings, additional amenities, and any other unique selling points.

The additional amenities you mention should be things your guests would actually need. Knowing your guests helps you target them specifically. It is all about knowing their wants and needs before they do. If your ideal guest is someone with young kids, you must know what they would want from a vacation rental. If you have a pool or body of water close by, you could provide toys for the kids to play with, flotation devices, and canoes. If your ideal client is a businessperson, they would want an office space with quiet surroundings and good Wi-Fi. Make sure you are able to provide these things, and you will have a better chance of landing quality guests.

TIPS FOR INCREASING VISIBILITY IN SEARCH

The Airbnb platform is competitive in nature. It has been designed to help guests find the perfect place to stay. This means all the properties are fighting for attention. Making it on the platform means you need to stand out from the crowd. Your property needs to show up among the first results in the search. How many times have you scrolled to the second or third page of Google's results? Probably never. The same works for the Airbnb platform. It functions like a search engine, and you need to show up high in the search results to make an impact and get the best chance of being seen.

Airbnb SEO

SEO stands for search engine optimization. This is key when using the platform because you want to rank highly in searches. Even if you have the perfect property, it isn't going to matter unless people can actually find you. You need to know what people are searching for, and then put that in your title and description. This comes back to identifying your ideal guest and then marketing to them directly. You will still appear in search results for other people, but knowing who your target market is makes it much more effective.

A great way to find out what words you should be using is to look at the most popular properties on Airbnb that are similar to yours. Look at how they describe their properties, and look at their reviews as well. Since you are offering something very similar to them, you are going after the same guests in the area. Knowing what has made them popular will give you some ideas for doing the same.

Be Reliable

Part of Airbnb SEO is using various techniques to be more reliable and show up more in searches. The right words are important, but so are many other factors. Airbnb wants its users to make the process smooth for their guests. This is to encourage people to keep coming back to the site. If guests have a terrible time on the site, then it will affect the platform and all the hosts. That is why they focus on rewarding reliable hosts who help guests have the best experience possible.

Replying to guests and making sure you do not cancel are two ways of doing this. You will be notified when you get a message, so you will be able to answer it as soon as possible. If you don't want to be active all the time, you can set a few times in the day when you handle messages and inquiries. This way, you are still able to answer all the questions and inquiries, but you are not stuck. As long as you are responding within twenty-four hours, you should be okay, but the faster and more responsive you are, the better.

Competitive Pricing

Again, Airbnb is a competitive market. This means everyone will be pricing their Airbnbs in order to attract as many guests as possible. Believe it or not, your place on the search page is impacted by the price you charge. Airbnb will not put the most expensive properties first because this might dishearten guests looking for an affordable stay. Have a look at the prices of the Airbnbs in your area that offer the same thing, and then price from there. This way, you know you're being fair, but you're also not undercharging. Charging too little might get you a spot on the first page of the Airbnb search engine, but you are going to be losing potential revenue. It is a balancing act.

Increase Available Booking Dates

The calendar on your Airbnb page is essential. It shows when your property is available to be booked and when it is full. If you do not have the Instant Booking function enabled, then you will need to log on and refresh your calendar manually every so often so that Airbnb knows that your calendar is accurate and updated.

Instant booking makes it much easier because guests can book without your approval. It makes things a whole lot easier for everybody involved when your calendar is updated automatically. You also have a higher chance of becoming a Superhost because your response rate will go up. You will find more guests interested in your listing, and you will show up more on their radar since many guests use the Instant Book filter.

After building an irresistible and visible listing, it's time to focus on building a strong reputation that draws guests in and keeps them coming back.

7

BUILDING A STRONG REPUTATION

"But brand is simply a collective impression some have about a product."

— ELON MUSK

Your reputation will follow you throughout your short-term rental journey. You will get repeat guests, and people will recommend you to their friends and family. When you have met all your guests' wants and needs and they have had an amazing stay, you will be surprised at how often you get referrals from them. It is a great way to continue getting your Airbnb booked as often as possible.

BECOMING A SUPERHOST

Becoming a Superhost is one of the best things you can do for your Airbnb business. It takes a while to become a Superhost, so it's not something that you can just start off with. Knowing how to become a Superhost is essential because you can start working on it from the beginning. It requires consistent work because even once you've gotten your Superhost status, you must continue working to ensure you retain it.

Let's first start by defining what a Superhost is. A Superhost is basically like a badge or award given to a host who is recognized for having great reviews and giving excellent guest experiences. You will get an orange badge on your listing to make sure people know that you are a Superhost. There are so many benefits to becoming a Superhost. You will get increased visibility as well as more trust from your guests. There is a filter on the search engine that allows a guest to filter out anyone who is not a Superhost. If they are looking for reliable and high-quality bookings, they will do this, and you will appear in a search.

You will need to hit a few milestones in order to become a Superhost. Your response rate will need to be above 90 percent, and you will need to have hosted guests ten times in the year or have 100 nights booked with three separate reservations. Your rating must be above 4.8, and 80 percent or more of your reviews must be five stars. The final criterion is that your cancellation rate be 1 percent or lower. Airbnb will assess and grant Superhost status every few months. Be patient because even if you don't get it, you can always try again. You can check your status on the Superhost tab of the platform. It makes it easier to see how far away you are from becoming a Superhost.

COLLECTING FIVE-STAR REVIEWS

Getting those five-star reviews is essential to becoming a Superhost. The more five-star reviews you have, the better your chances are of becoming a Superhost, and you will attract more guests. Once you become a Superhost, it is easier to maintain it because you are used to putting in the effort. The first thing you need to do is make sure that your Airbnb is of good quality, comfortable, and clean. Many people get bad reviews because of the inferior cleanliness of their Airbnb. You are in direct competition with hotels, so you need to make sure that it is justified for people to book with you rather than a hotel with professional staff. You might want to hire a professional cleaner who can look over the property and clean it well. If professional cleaners are not in your budget right now, you can create a cleaning checklist for yourself to make sure that you do not miss anything.

One of the biggest mistakes that Airbnb hosts make is that they oversell their listings. If you make your property seem so amazing that meeting those standards is unrealistic, then you will not get good reviews. You need to put your best foot forward when it comes to your listing, but you also need to be honest and accurate. This way, when your guests check-in, they know what to expect, but it's also easier for you to exceed expectations and get a better review. For example, you don't have to mention there will be a welcome box or basket waiting for them. However, they will have a welcome surprise when they see this waiting for them when they check in. This enhances their experience and makes it more likely that they will give you a good review.

At the end of their stay, make sure to ask them for a review. Many guests have a great time but don't leave a review; this is a missed opportunity. Sometimes, just asking is the push they need to give you that review. If you are there when they check out, you have a better chance of connecting with them. You can ask them if they have any feedback or if there is anything negative you need to change for the next time. This way, there is a lower chance of them simply leaving a bad review if they aren't happy with something. You can reassure them that you will make the changes. You can also offer them a discount on their next stay or something similar to apologize. Explaining to them that good reviews are essential for your business means you are more likely to get their review. If they were unhappy with their stay, do not suggest they give you a review. Otherwise, it could turn out badly for you.

On the Airbnb platform, you can review your guests. This will let other Airbnb hosts know whether they should allow a booking from this type of guest. This is also a great way to prompt your guests to review you. If a guest has been a good guest, make sure you give them a positive review. For guests whose experiences were less than ideal, it's important to provide an honest and appropriate review reflecting their stay.

ENCOURAGING REPEAT GUESTS

Getting some repeat guests is really going to help with your profit, as well as make your property management easier. When you have a trusted repeat guest, you know that your property is going to be in good hands, and there will be lower marketing costs. You don't have to worry about trying to fill empty spaces because you know your guests are going to come back. This leads to a more secure and stable income, and you can build relationships and trust with your guests.

Welcome Them

First impressions really do matter a lot when you are running an Airbnb. If they have booked with you, it means that you have made a good first impression online, and now it's time to carry this through by making a good impression in person. Meeting your guests and introducing yourself is a great way to do this. It helps to establish a personal relationship with them. You can show them around and let them know that you'll be available for whatever they need. It makes many guests feel secure to know that they can put a face to the name they have been communicating with. Don't worry if you can't be available in person to meet your guest at check-in. We will cover remote check-in in the next chapter.

On the property, make sure that you have provided the basic necessities, but also try to go above and beyond. Surprising your guests with small things can really go a long way. A bottle of wine and some homemade treats can make all the difference. Also, make sure to stock things like toilet paper, fridge essentials, and other bathroom essentials so they don't have to worry about going out to find and buy these items. If they have forgotten something at home, it is already taken care of, and they can enjoy their vacation. Think about what your hotel or Airbnb offers you when you stay over. What would've made your stay smoother and more enjoyable?

Keep in Touch

Once they are ready to check out, make sure you meet them and receive the keys, so you can have a conversation with them and wish them well on their way. If you are unable to meet with your guests, don't worry too much about it now. We will cover other ways to stay in contact a bit later in the book.

This is also a great time to get any feedback and reassure them that you will be implementing it in the future. This way, it instills some excitement, so they will want to come back to see how you have improved your Airbnb.

You can also send them an email the day after they check out to thank them for staying with you. At this point, you may want to ask for a review. Once you get the review, make sure that you reply to it, whether it is positive or negative. For a positive review, you can simply thank them and let them know you are excited for the next time they stay with you. If it is a negative review, you can address the points they are concerned about and let them know that you will make the changes accordingly.

Give a Discount

Everybody loves a discount. One of the best ways to encourage people to rebook with you is to give them a discount for the next time they stay. Your discounts don't have to be for busy times. You can set these discounts or specials for times when you know bookings are typically slower. This way, you encourage people to book at those points, but you also offer them a discount, so they are incentivized to do that. They will be happy, and you will benefit from it as well.

You might even consider creating some sort of loyalty program, if it works for you. You can create an email list of all of your previous guests during the slow period. Simply send out an email with the discount exclusive to them. You would be surprised at how many people will jump at the chance to stay at an Airbnb they truly enjoy for a cheaper rate.

Your reputation is essential when it comes to building a sustainable Airbnb business. The good news is that if you do these few things, you can get there. Having established a strong reputation, let's now turn to one of the fundamental notions that underlies everything we've discussed so far: communication.

Leveling Up Airbnb Properties Across the Board

"Alone we can do so little; together we can do so much."

— HELEN KELLER

Take a moment now to think about yourself as a guest rather than an owner. If you were thorough in your research, you probably stayed in a good number of Airbnbs before you started listing yours... How many did you see had room for improvement?

Of course, every Airbnb owner wants their property to stand out from the crowd... But we also want to raise the quality of Airbnbs across the board and make our own stays (and booking experiences!) as guests more enjoyable – and this is part of my hope with this book.

So while your brain is busy thinking through all the ways you can maximize your property's potential, I'd like to ask you to take a moment to help other Airbnb owners level up their game.

That's as easy as leaving a short review – just as you want happy guests to do when they leave your property.

By leaving a review of this book on Amazon, you'll show other Airbnb owners where they can find the guidance they need to get the most out of their property – and, in the process, you'll help raise the standard across the board.

Simply by letting other readers know how this book has helped you and what they'll find inside, you'll show them where they can find everything they need to make sure their property is fulfilling its true potential as an Airbnb destination.

Thank you so much for your support. Now, let's get back to it!

Scan the QR code below

8

MASTERING GUEST COMMUNICATION

One study found that 72 percent of complaints on Twitter were the result of poor customer service (Kemmis, 2022). Another 22 percent were related to scams, but we are not in the business of running scams, so this should not happen. A lot of poor customer service or unmet expectations come down to communication. If you communicate to your guests exactly what they will be receiving and everybody's on the same page, then there will be a much lower likelihood of complaints. Knowing how to properly communicate with your guests is a valuable skill when running any kind of property rental business.

AUTOMATING GUEST MESSAGES

When it comes to communication, there are a few very standard questions and concerns that are always brought up. Sometimes, this is specific to your Airbnb, and other times, it is a general question. As you spend longer in the business, you will realize what the most common queries and concerns are. This makes it a lot easier for you to develop a communication standard because you know exactly what is going to be asked.

When you are communicating with your guests, it is so important that you be transparent and available to talk to them. Many hosts want to sell their property as the best place on earth. That is understandable, but the truth is that you are setting up your guests to be disappointed. If they tell you they want a quiet location because they want to rest and relax, you might have the urge to sell your property as the perfect place for that. However, if your property is right next to a highway or close to an amusement park, you know that it's not a quiet area. While you may reassure the guests that your property is perfect for their needs, when they get there and realize there are children running around or cars driving past every five minutes, it's going to be an issue. You may get a negative review and some very unhappy guests.

Most guests are pretty forgiving when they know what to expect and when you are honest with them. Communicating well helps protect you and manage their expectations. If you have communicated something to them, then you can always go back to the conversation and show them what was agreed upon. Any important communication should always be done through email or some other kind of written medium. This way, there is a trackable history, so either of you can go back and ensure the other one is holding up their end of the bargain.

Some guests will want to communicate all the time, and others won't bother with it. Either way, it is important to make sure that the line of communication is open. There are specific moments when you should make yourself available to communicate with your guests. Firstly, it's going to be when they make an inquiry about booking with you. This is when they will have the most questions, and you should be available to answer them. Once they have booked, it is a good idea to send a message thanking them for booking with you and letting them know you are available to answer any questions or address their comments if they have any. The day before or the day of their arrival, you should send them a message to make sure they know the basics, such as the directions and check-in details, so everything goes smoothly for them. After they have checked in and are settled, you might want to check in after the first night to ask if everything has gone well and if they need anything. Once they have checked out, you can continue communication a few days after they depart to make sure they enjoyed their stay.

If you are the one who initiates most of the communication, it means that you have more control over what is going on. It is much better to be the one in control of the conversation because there is a lower likelihood of arguments and misunderstandings on your end. Sometimes, guests forget to communicate until the last minute, and then it is very difficult for you to meet their needs.

Being on point with communication can be quite difficult, especially if you are busy. This is where automated messages come in handy. You only have to create message templates, which you can copy and paste into your message field. Airbnb has a saved message feature, which makes it a lot easier. You can create as many saved messages as you would like for every occasion. You can create templates for the most commonly asked questions, booking confirmations, and welcome messages. This means that you can effectively communicate without actually having to do much.

Another option is to use a third-party site where you can completely automate the messages. This means that you don't even have to click and send the messages since it will be done on your behalf. You will have a saved message template on the software, and when specific events pop up, the right message will be sent to your guest. You could have messages for check-in and checkout, booking inquiries, booking confirmations, and cancellations. This way, the information is sent to your guests, and everybody receives the same type of communication. If there is something specific that the guest contacts you about, they can do so, as there will always be this option. Remember that even automated messages cannot cover every situation. Sometimes, speaking to your guest is going to be the best way to understand what they need or what their concerns are. Automated messages make your life a little bit easier because you don't have to continuously communicate the same thing repeatedly.

CHECK-IN OPTIONS: IN-PERSON OR REMOTE

When it comes to checking into an Airbnb, there are typically two options. The first is an in-person check-in where you, as the host, will go to meet your guests and check them in. This allows you to connect with your guests face-to-face and meet them. You will be able to show them the Airbnb and guide them through any rules or expectations, or even assist them with certain things if needed. Many hosts prefer an in-person check-in because you get to build this personal connection. They feel as though it gives them a better chance of receiving a higher review.

Remote or self-check-in options have become more popular since they are more convenient for both the host and the guest. With self-check-in, you would need to install a key lock box or smart lock on your Airbnb. A key lock box is simply a box in which you place the key that you lock using a code. You would then give the guest the code so they could access the key. With a smart lock, they would use a code to open the door of the Airbnb in order to get access. You would change the code for each new guest to enhance safety. Once the guest checks out, you can change the code so they no longer have access to the property.

This is definitely a less personal way to check in. However, there are many benefits to it. Doing an in-person check-in means that you have to be available at a certain time to check the guests in. This can be incredibly inconvenient, and if the guests are late or something unexpected happens, then you could potentially be wasting a lot of time. From the guest's perspective, it means they are limited to a specific time when they can check in and check out. Only when you are available to come and check them in and out will they be able to do so.

This lack of flexibility makes the process a bit more difficult for everyone involved.

When using the self-check-in option, you need to ensure the communication is on point throughout the whole process. You will not have the opportunity to talk to your guests when they check in. This means you should send your guests a message or an email with detailed check-in instructions to smooth the process. Make sure they know what the code is and how to unlock the lock box or use the smart lock. You should still be on standby, just in case something goes wrong and they need your assistance. No technology is fully proven, so it is important to be available should something happen.

On top of all of this, you also need to make sure your guests know how to use the items in the home so they are not confused about anything. Things that you may think are common knowledge might not be for them. Since you are not there to answer their questions, having detailed instructions is really helpful. Make a book or pamphlet with instructions for the different technologies and electronics in the house. You might also want to place instruction sheets next to the relevant electronics and appliances. This does not have to be in an email since this can be in the actual home and will make it easier for them to know what instructions are for what thing.

You would also want to send them clear checkout instructions. You can do this with the check-in email you sent them, but you can also remind them when they check out. This should make things a lot smoother for them since it is easy to forget when on vacation. You will definitely have to be more intentional with your communication when you allow self-check-in, but it does make things a lot easier. You also have the opportunity to get better reviews because your guests can handle the process smoothly. As long as the communication before and during this day has been good, you don't have to worry about getting negative reviews for not being there in person for check-in. In fact, many people prefer a self-check-in, as it is a lot quicker and allows them to check in early in the morning or late in the evening if they need to.

DEALING WITH PROBLEM GUESTS

The dreaded problem guest! If you have been in the Airbnb business for a while, you have probably had a run-in with a problem guest. This is someone who is just a bad Airbnb guest and causes unnecessary issues for you. The good news is that most Airbnb guests tend to take care of the property and obey the rules. However, a small percentage of them can cause huge difficulties for you.

Learning how to deal with these guests is essential to running your Airbnb business. At the end of the day, a guest is a guest, and you want to handle the situation properly so you don't get any negative reviews. On top of that, you want to deliver excellent service as much as is within your control. This may mean you have to go a little above and beyond what you normally would to de-escalate the situation and make sure your guest is happy.

Instant Book is a great function because it allows a guest to book without you needing to confirm. It makes the whole process a lot easier, but there is a catch. When you manually confirm an Airbnb booking, you get to check their profile to see if there are any red flags. Instant Book does not allow this. If you are worried about getting a problem guest, you might consider turning off the Instant Book function and just making sure that you are on point with guest inquiries and confirming bookings. It is also important to note that reviews tend to be subjective, which means that you have to use your discretion. Sometimes, a host might give a guest a bad review that wasn't warranted in the first place. However, it is a good idea to be cautious of guests who do have negative reviews.

The next thing you need to do is make sure that your house rules are clearly laid out. Indicate that by staying at your Airbnb, they agree to the rules and terms of doing so. This means you can hold them liable for not following the rules you have established. In many cases, it is not that the guest is disrespectful, but you must remember that you could get people from various cultures, cities, and countries. The way they do things may be completely different from the way you do them. This is why you need to make sure that your expectations are clear so that everybody's on the same page. The rules that you sent out should be easy to understand and simple so there is no miscommunication. You will need to communicate this upon booking and then again when checking in. If they do not agree or don't like the rules, they simply will not stay with you, and you have avoided a bad situation.

If you encounter a situation where a guest is breaking the rules or causing a problem, you will need to deal with it directly. Many times, it could be a case of miscommunication or them simply not understanding. It is always best to communicate directly with your guests rather than getting other people involved. In many cases, you will be able to come to some agreement and move past the situation. In a dispute or disagreement, it can be easy to go on the defensive, but it's important not to blame or judge a guest. That could turn out badly for you, so handling the situation diplomatically is essential. Understand where they are coming from and what they need. It is usually best to be flexible to find a solution to the issue a guest is facing. You can offer solutions, and usually, you will come to some sort of middle ground or agreement. The main goal is to make sure your guest does not get overly emotional or upset. This could lead to irrational behavior that can be difficult to de-escalate. You need to be the calm and stable one, and if you feel that things are getting out of control, it may be best to take a step back and come back to the conversation in a few minutes. You can always talk to someone else if you need to vent, but make sure that this does not happen when you are with the guest.

If you end up in a situation where there is no middle ground and the guest is simply not listening, then you can escalate it to Airbnb. They are usually good at handling these situations. If it is a terrible situation where there may be legal issues, then you could possibly get the authorities involved. However, this is a very rare case, so you shouldn't be too concerned about that. Just remember that having the guests' best interests in mind is going to help you deal with any situation that arises in the most constructive way possible. It gives you the best chance of having a happy guest while still sticking to your standards. It might be a good option even if you have to make a few compromises until the guest leaves. You can then never allow that guest to book with you in the future, so you will not need to deal with the situation again.

Mastering communication is just one aspect of running a successful Airbnb. It allows you to make sure that you and your guests are on the same page. This will give your guests a better experience and ensure your standards are met. But how can you manage all these tasks without consuming your entire day?

9

AUTOMATION AND TIME MANAGEMENT

Automation is the future of Airbnb because it makes the entire process a lot easier for the host. When you are an Airbnb host, you will have to do quite a few things on repeat. This can get quite tedious and, frankly, annoying. Finding ways to automate these aspects makes the process easier for you so you can focus on other things. Automation is especially important for those who have multiple properties.

AUTOMATING RULESETS

When you have multiple listings on Airbnb, you can access certain Pro Tools features. This allows you to create pricing and availability rules that can be saved and applied to all or some of your listings. It makes it a lot easier to run your Airbnb business because you don't have to keep doing the same things over and over again. Let's dive a little bit deeper into rule sets and how they work. A rule set is basically a set of parameters and rules for a specific action or thing. You will be able to name your rule set and then set the rules for how you would like things to change based on those rules.

Let's say you want to create a rule set for your nightly price. You could set a rule for adjusting the price per night based on the time of year. Your price could decrease by 10 percent during the weekdays or during low travel seasons. You may also want to create a rule set where a discount is automatically applied if the guest stays longer than a certain number of days. Other rule sets you could use are to give last-minute discounts as the day draws closer or an early bird discount if they book well in advance. You can also set things like check-in and checkout requirements, where you choose the days that a guest is able to do this. You can then apply your rule set to one or all of your listings, and it will change your current pricing and availability settings based on that.

The rules will only be applied when needed. If you have set a rule that there is a 20 percent discount on last-minute bookings, the 20 percent discount will automatically be applied to your pricing as the day draws nearer. You won't have to do anything; it will just automatically change on the Airbnb platform. When somebody books at the last minute, they will get this discounted rate. You don't have to worry about manually changing the pricing.

Using rule sets makes things so much easier. When you have multiple properties, it becomes very difficult to track exactly what is going on. You will have bookings for certain days and times based on the property, so this means there are multiple calendars to manage. You will probably be using a similar strategy across all of your properties, so using a rule set means that you don't have to be actively involved. You can develop your strategy and then just implement it across the board. You can also set rules for specific properties if you have different strategies for each one.

SCHEDULING AND AUTOMATING GUEST CHECK-INS

We touched on self-check-in in the previous chapter. This is a form of automating guest check-ins, so you don't have to be available in order for your guests to check into the Airbnb or check out when their stay is done. First, you will need to ensure you have the right equipment to automate the check-in process. This means you'll need either a smart lock, keypad, or lock box so your guests can get into the property.

The type of tool you use for self-check-in depends on your budget and what you feel is going to work best for you. Lock boxes are a pretty inexpensive way to do the self-check-in process. You'll just need to purchase a lock box and mount it on the wall near the property entrance. You will then program the lock box with a specific code that you will give to your guest on the day of check-in. They will enter the code and access the key when they arrive.

Another option is a smart lock, which is very secure and convenient. You do not need physical keys in order to use a smart lock, so it means you will have to replace the current lock with a new one. There are some smart locks that will attach to the lock that's already on the door. You will provide your guests with a passcode, and they can just enter it in order to access the house. This is actually a great option because it also eliminates the risk of the guest losing a key. These locks are great because you can integrate other software into them, such as being sent an automated message when guests check in. This message can be used to welcome guests to the property and give them relevant information about whatever is in the home.

Once you have your automated check-in set up, you just need to ensure the process is smooth for your guests. You are not going to be there to take care of them, so making sure the process is smooth is essential. You can set up a welcome box so they can easily find it as soon as they enter the Airbnb. This can be everything they need for their stay. You can have a guidebook or a house manual. This will have all the relevant information they need on this day, as well as how to use the electronics and appliances. You should also add things like the rules, Wi-Fi details, emergency contact information, and recommendations of things they can do in and around the area. This will make the guest feel a lot more at home and at ease.

Since you are not going to be there, it is important to make the welcome feel personal to them. Adding a few personal touches always goes a long way toward making them feel special and welcome. Providing a bottle of local wine or fresh flowers in the vase are nice touches that really add to the welcome experience. If the area is well known for a specific type of food or snack, then you can place these in a basket or on the counter so they can get the full experience of the area.

It is always a good idea to send your guests a checkup message at some point during their stay. This can be done in the morning after they check in because they will be settled. At this point, they might have a few questions, and you would be able to provide them with the answers. It helps them connect with you and shows you are an attentive host, even though you have not met them personally. You can automate this messaging process as well so you do not forget.

AUTOMATING OR OUTSOURCING CLEANING AND MAINTENANCE

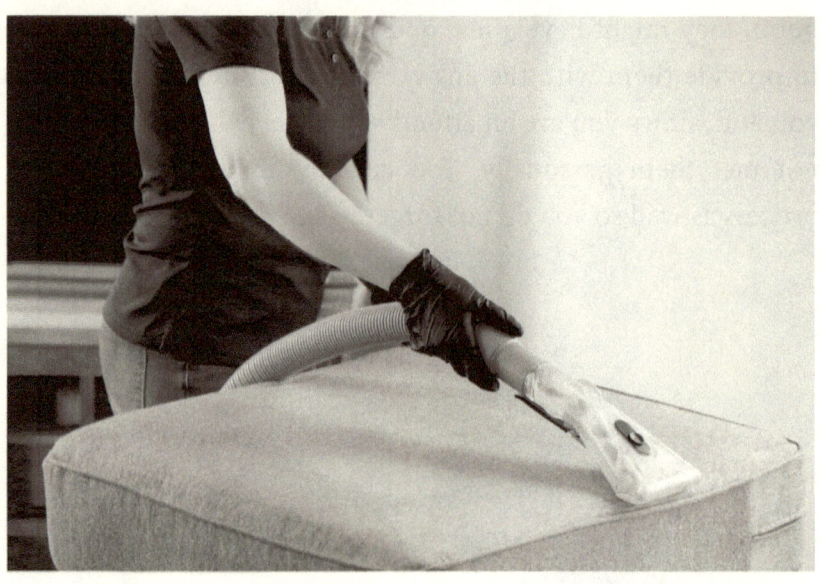

Keeping your Airbnb clean and well-maintained is crucial if you want your guests to have a good experience. If you look through reviews on Airbnb, most of the negative ones come because the house has not been well-maintained or is dirty. Cleaning and maintenance should always be at the top of your priority list, and they need to be done thoroughly so that every guest has an amazing time at your rental. If you have ever stayed at a dirty hotel, you know how uncomfortable it can be. You do not want your guests to feel the same way when they stay at your Airbnb.

As far as we have come with technology, we do not have automatic or robot cleaners just yet. Even if you do try to use some sort of robot or technology to clean, there's no guarantee that it will get everything done. You still need a human being to go in and check to make sure the property is clean and up to standard. The good news is that you have many tools at your disposal when it comes to automating your Airbnb cleaning and maintenance.

The first thing you want to do is hire a professional cleaner who will be able to get into your Airbnb and clean regularly. You can hire one from a company or go online to find one. You might even know a few professional cleaners personally, and it will make it easier to trust them if you do. It is important to get a reliable cleaner who is going to do the job well. The whole point of automating your cleaning processes is that you don't have to be involved. You want to be able to trust the cleaner, as you don't want to be called on by your guests with complaints.

If you have found a good and reliable cleaner, you will need to train them. Every Airbnb host and person has different requirements for their properties. You need to make sure that you and the cleaner are on the same page when it comes to this. One of the best ways to do this is to create a cleaning checklist. Remember that the requirements for cleaning a vacation rental are different from cleaning a regular home. When it comes to an Airbnb, it is best that the cleaner goes above and beyond to make sure that it is completely spotless. Create a checklist for each room so it's easy for the cleaner to go through it and get things done. In my previous book, *How to Set Up and Run a Successful Airbnb Business*, we go through exactly how to get your Airbnb spotless and the aspects that many people overlook.

The cleaner should also be responsible for restocking the property for the next guest. This means they should have access to your inventory, so you need to have an inventory tracking process in place. This way, you know when you need to go out and buy more inventory and can make sure nothing goes missing. You can create a checklist on an app or even use a spreadsheet. You can make a list of everything that is in the inventory, as well as how many of each product there are. When the cleaner is restocking, they will simply update the spreadsheet to show the current number you have. When the numbers start getting low, then it's time for you to go shopping to replace the inventory. It is best to leave all the products in a place on the property where your guests cannot reach them, but your cleaner can easily access them. A locked cupboard or room tends to be a good option.

Now that you have all of this set up, it is important to make sure that the cleaner knows exactly when they need to go in and clean. This means they need access to your booking calendar. This way, they're able to see when people are checking out and when they're checking in. Make sure the booking calendar is as detailed as possible and includes the times your guests will be checking in and out. On the day of checkout or the day after, the cleaner will go in and clean the property as instructed. If there are any changes, you can communicate directly with the cleaner, but for the most part, the process should be completely automated.

On top of regular cleaning, you should also schedule deep-cleaning. This is especially necessary when you have many guests staying back-to-back at your property. Regular cleaning may not suffice, and there are always things that you need to get into. You can schedule this deep-cleaning when there is an empty space in the calendar. The cleaner can go in and take care of a few in-depth things related to cleaning and maintenance. This is actually incredibly valuable because it will help identify anything that needs to be replaced or maintained. Your cleaner can communicate with you if something has broken or is perishing. You will then have the information to go in and replace or fix it. These deep-cleaning sessions should happen once every few months, depending on how busy your Airbnb has been.

There is specific software that deals with this entire process to make things easier for you. It can automatically connect you with a cleaner and update your calendar on both ends so everybody knows what needs to be done. One of these apps is called "Turno," and it will handle everything for you. It is worth looking into.

Even though the entire process is going to be automated, it is still important that you be involved at some level. You will need to go in and check the property to make sure that the standards have remained the same. You don't have to do this often, especially if you trust your cleaner. However, doing spot checks every few weeks or months is always a good thing. If something needs to be changed or you want the cleaning strategy to shift a little, then you can do that or identify the problem when you are there. Overall, automating your cleaning makes everything so much easier and gives you a lot more time to focus on building a business and doing other things.

Automation and efficient time management are the backbone of a successful Airbnb business. Knowing how to do this effectively will make your life much easier. You will be saving so much time and effort. Another crucial aspect is making smart financial decisions, which we will cover in the next chapter.

10

FINANCIAL CONSIDERATIONS

Regardless of the type of business you have, it is very important to have a good financial strategy. This will help you take your business to the next level and ensure that your profit margins are as large as they can be. If you don't have a financial strategy, you can end up losing money in areas that you weren't even thinking of. A simple plan allows you to keep yourself organized and make sure that you are taking steps to reach a specific goal.

CHOOSING THE RIGHT CANCELLATION POLICIES

Multiple cancellation policies are available on the Airbnb platform, which is great. Choosing the right cancellation policy can have an impact on your finances. If you allow your guests to cancel up until the day they check in, this means that they do not have to pay, and it is highly unlikely that you will get somebody else to fill in that spot. This results in a loss of income. Another thing to consider is that if your cancellation policy is way too strict, people aren't going to want to book since there is no flexibility. Again, this could result in a loss of income.

Let's talk a little bit about your options when it comes to cancellation policies. Once you set up your listing on the Airbnb platform, you'll be asked to choose a cancellation policy, and there will be a brief description of what it would entail. Airbnb can change how they set up their cancellation policies, so it is always best to make sure that your information is up-to-date. However, we are going to go through the basics here so that you fully understand and can start thinking about your cancellation policy strategy.

The cancellation policies are divided into two categories. These are standard and long-term policies. You will use the standard policy when you are using your Airbnb to allow people to stay for short-term reservations. This would be less than twenty-eight consecutive nights. Long-term policies would be anything more than that, and they would override standard policy.

Underneath the category of standard policies, you have four cancellation policies. The first is a flexible cancellation policy where a guest can cancel up to twenty-four hours before the day and time of check-in. If they do that, then they will get a refund. If they cancel less than twenty-four hours before check-in, then you will be paid for the first night, but if they cancel after the check-in day, you will be paid for every night plus an additional one.

The moderate cancellation policy allows the guest to cancel up to five days before they check in. If they do this, then they will get a full refund, but if they cancel after that, you will be paid 50 percent for all nights booked that they didn't stay, plus an additional night. If they decide to stay for part of the booked nights, you'll get paid in full for each night they stay.

The firm cancellation policy entitles the guest to a full refund if they cancel more than 30 days before check-in. If they cancel between seven and thirty days before, then you will get 50 percent for all nights they have booked. If they cancel less than seven days before they are required to check in, you'll get 100 percent of the rate for every night. They are entitled to a full refund if they cancel within forty-eight hours of booking, but this only applies if they do so at least 14 days before they check in.

Next, we have a strict cancellation policy, which means that you will get 50 percent returned for all booked nights if they cancel between seven and fourteen days before they check in. If they cancel after that, you will be entitled to 100 percent of the nights. If they want a full refund, they will need to cancel within forty-eight hours of booking, which needs to be done at least fourteen days before the check-in date.

For long-term policies, you have two different cancellation policies. This is a firm, long-term cancellation policy where the guest can receive a refund if they cancel a minimum of thirty days before the check-in date. If they fail to do this, then you will get 100 percent for every night they spend at your Airbnb, plus thirty additional nights. If fewer than thirty nights remain on the reservation at the time and the guest decides to cancel, you'll get 100 percent of the remaining nights. The next policy is a strict long-term cancellation policy where the guest can be refunded if they cancel the reservation within forty-eight hours of booking, but this must be at least twenty-eight days before the date of check-in. If the guest does not abide by this, then you will get paid for every night booked, plus thirty additional nights from when they canceled. If the guest decides to cancel with less than thirty days remaining on the reservation, then you'll still get paid 100 percent for the nights remaining.

The type of cancellation policy you choose is totally up to you, but you should bear in mind that it has consequences. You will definitely attract more people with a more flexible cancellation policy. People won't feel like they are locked into something they are not sure they can commit to. Many Airbnb hosts choose a flexible cancellation policy since that generally attracts more guests. However, if you notice this does not work for you, then you can bump it up to a strict cancellation policy. This will protect your finances and make sure that you have enough time to fill the spots should someone cancel.

UNDERSTANDING THE ADDITIONAL FEES

There are multiple additional fees that can be added on when you have an Airbnb. This means there are other sources of income besides the accommodation rate you will be charging. This is a really important concept because you want to make sure you are maximizing your profit. Now, you don't want to just charge without a purpose. That can be really annoying for a guest. However, you should look at what you can charge or what additional services you can offer to your guests.

Cleaning Fees

This is a fee that you add on for the cleaning and turning over of your Airbnb. It is a one-time fee that the guest will pay. Typically, it will be included in the price the guest pays when they book. Since this is a one-time fee, it will be split over the days your guests book. So if your guests book for four nights, then the cleaning fee will be divided by four and added to each night's rate. This means that your guests will not be shocked when they go to pay and notice a fee added on.

Since the fee is added to the overall price, guests are able to filter the listing by the overall price, including fees. It gives them a more accurate idea of what they will be paying for their stay. You can charge whatever you would like as a cleaning fee. Just make sure you are not going overboard. Recently, Airbnb guests have not been happy about the cleaning fee. It is a good idea to keep an eye out on social media to see what people are saying so you know if there is a change to be made.

Some hosts prefer not to charge a cleaning fee and simply increase the nightly rate. This can work, but if you get shorter stays, you might not make enough to cover the cost of the cleaning. You also don't want to increase your nightly price so much that it becomes unreasonable for most people. A cleaning fee is just a one-time expense, so there is no danger of that.

You will need to decide how much to charge based on your property. A bigger house with multiple rooms and bathrooms should have a higher cleaning fee than a one-bedroom apartment. The average is about $50–$75, but averages can be misleading. Rather, have a look at the competition and see what they are charging. Remember to only look at properties similar to yours. This will give you an accurate idea. Another way to work out the cleaning fee is, if you use a cleaning company, to determine the company's fee. All you have to do is charge the company fee plus a little more for supplies, and that will be the cleaning fee.

Additional Guest Fees

When you set up your Airbnb listing, you get to set the initial prices and how many people it will sleep. However, you can also charge for an additional person. Sometimes, there is an unexpected guest joining them, or they have a small child who doesn't need that much space. It is important to note that your property will still have a maximum capacity and cannot accommodate more than a certain number. Sure, a person could potentially sleep on the couch, but when a guest is paying a fee, they may not be happy with that.

An extra person is an extra cost for you. Even if you don't have to add any extra furniture to accommodate them, there are utility costs, the use of toiletries, and more wear and tear. It is important to consider these things. You also don't want to charge too much for an additional person. The guest is already paying for the Airbnb. You can have a look at what your competitors are charging before you decide on your price. If you notice that the majority of your competitors are not charging this fee, it might be best to skip it. When people go to book and see a fee has been applied, they may be turned off and look for another place to stay. The fee is added to the price they see, so they should be happy with how much they are paying before they go to checkout. However, there is a breakdown of what they are paying for at the end, and this can simply turn people off when they see fees.

Pet Fees

It is becoming more common for people to travel with their furry friends. This means that if you do not allow pets at all, it could end up hurting your bottom line. This is especially true if you have an outdoor type of property where dogs are able to get out and explore, or people can take them for walks. It is important to note that you will not be able to collect fees on service animals. In most cases, a service animal does not include emotional support animals, so you are able to charge for them. Make sure you check the laws in your area. For example, New York and California prohibit charging for emotional support animals.

You will be able to charge a flat fee for the pet. This will cover additional cleaning and maintenance due to having a pet in the home. You can charge per pet or have one fee for all. It is up to you. You will need to decide what fee is going to work for you, but remember to not charge too much. Around $25–$100 seems to be the average, but it depends on your property. Bigger properties can charge more since there is more to clean.

There are risks to allowing pets. Not everyone has well-trained pets. On top of that, people have different rules for their pets. If you are allowing pets in your Airbnb, then it is a good idea to have some rules and guidelines for people to follow. Mention any areas or rooms that pets would not be allowed to enter, and if you don't want pets on the furniture, make sure to mention it. With this being said, it can be difficult to enforce since you just don't know what goes on when you are not there.

By now, you've gotten a firm grasp on the financial aspects of running an Airbnb business. Yet, maximizing profits isn't just about getting your pricing and fees right; it's also about ensuring you attract enough bookings in the first place.

11

INNOVATIVE STRATEGIES FOR BOOSTING BOOKINGS

"Innovation distinguishes between a leader and a follower."

— STEVE JOBS

Figuring out how to boost bookings is incredibly important. It can help you increase your income, possibly even double it. The good news is that many of these strategies do not even require that much effort or more money. You will need to put in some additional work, but the profit you can get from this is definitely worth it. You don't have to do everything in this chapter. Rather, look at what is realistic for you and what you can actually maintain. You still want to give the best service and quality to your guests.

SWITCHING TO PER-ROOM LISTING

Last-minute bookings can really help you increase your overall income. There are many people who choose to book at the last minute because of unexpected circumstances, so you can take advantage of this. In most cases, people who are booking last minute are not coming in large groups or large families. When a family or a group of people go on vacation, they typically have to plan in advance so everybody's schedule matches up. If you have a large property that can hold multiple people, you might be missing out on the last-minute booking market.

Thankfully, there is a way to still get into this market without buying an entirely new and smaller property. All you have to do is switch from renting out an entire home to a per-room listing. You have the option to divide up your property so that more people can stay at your Airbnb. If you have four bedrooms in your Airbnb, you can rent it out to four people. A single person or a couple who is looking for a last-minute booking would be happy to stay in this kind of arrangement since it would be cheaper. You would need to make your nightly rate lower than what it is for an entire property. Have a look at what people are charging in the area for one-bedroom apartments or per-room listings.

PET-FRIENDLY PROPERTIES

As mentioned in the previous chapter, there are many people who love to bring their furry friends along with them when they go on vacation. When you have an Airbnb, your main goal is to try to appeal to as large a population as possible. This will help you find a large number of guests who are willing to stay with you and pay your rates.

People who want to bring their pets are usually willing to pay a little more since fewer pet-friendly places are on the market. They are more likely to stay in an Airbnb rather than a hotel because there is more space. It is also usually cheaper to bring the pet along rather than book them into a kennel or hire someone to go to the house to feed and take care of it.

When you offer a pet-friendly listing, you'll need to make sure that the home is pet-proof. Just as people babyproof their homes, the same applies to pets. If you have any fancy little trinkets and delicate items in the home, it is best to remove them, as you don't want these things to break. You may also need to change your house rules to include pets. There might also be limitations on the type of pet that is allowed. For example, if you have a small apartment, someone would not be able to bring a large dog. You can put weight and size restrictions on the type of pet that you allow on your property. You should also stipulate that the pets who stay should be well-trained and housebroken. This should minimize the number of accidents that happen.

It is also important that you highlight the type of pet that is allowed on your property. Even though cats and dogs are the most common pets, not everybody has them. There are some exotic pets and some that are not traditional. If you're not happy to have these in your home, then stipulate the type of pet that will be allowed. In general, if you just allow dogs, you should cover most of the people who want to bring their pets along with them.

Having a specific section for pet rules in your guest book and on your listing is a good idea. This will help the guests know exactly what is expected of them and add some security for you so you can protect your property. Things that may seem common sense to you might not be for other people, so it is important to be very specific with your rules. Highlight areas where the pets may not be permitted to enter, and state whether you allow them to be on the furniture. Make sure you have stipulated how to get rid of dog poop and cat litter. You will also need to indicate how they should keep the property clean.

Next, you need to move on to making your rental pet-friendly. When you advertise as a pet-friendly place, you need to make sure that the pets feel just as comfortable as the people. You can provide things like food and water bowls, a dog bed, toys, and a litter box or litter pick-up bags. If there are areas that are off-limits to pets, then install some fencing or gates to cordon off these areas. Another good idea is to have removable and washable covers for the furniture. This is important because even if dogs and cats are not allowed on the furniture, there is no guarantee they won't be. On top of that, they could easily rub against the furniture and cause stains and smells to stick. If the next person to check in has allergies or dislikes animals, they might be offended and unhappy with dog hair on the furniture. Easily removable and washable covers mean that you can keep things clean. Remember, you are trying to include a lot of different guests and not isolate yourself to just a pet-friendly Airbnb.

Another thing you can do is charge a higher security deposit and cleaning fee when people bring their pets along. The risk of breakage is a lot higher when there are pets, and most pet owners are aware of this. Charging high-security deposits means you are protected and will have the money to replace something if it breaks. If nothing happens, you can simply give back the security deposit, and nothing is lost on the guests' part. You can only charge a security deposit if connected through an API. We will talk more about this later on.

It is also really important that you get the property thoroughly cleaned after pets have been in it. Even if you only allow families with pets to stay at your Airbnb, making sure it's clean for the next person is essential. Animals can get worked up if too many scents of different dogs and cats are on the property. Invest in some good cleaning products that will help remove any odors. These can be a little bit more expensive, and that's why you charge a slightly higher cleaning fee.

RENTAL ARBITRAGE

Airbnb continues to expand. This means that more people do want to get into it. Whether you are thinking of getting into Airbnb or you already have a property, you can take part in rental arbitrage. It allows you to get into property rentals without actually owning property. It makes it a lot cheaper to get started, so you can increase your income.

The basics of rental arbitrage are to simply rent a property and then sublet it on the Airbnb platform. We all know that purchasing a property can be incredibly expensive, and it is becoming less and less realistic for people to do so. Growing your Airbnb business in this way means you can build a mechanism to increase your cash flow without actually owning your property and putting down a huge amount of money to get started.

You will essentially be using the income from your Airbnb to pay off the rent every month. If you play your cards right, you will be able to make quite a big profit from doing this. Now, you have to make sure that your landlord is happy for you to do this. Some landlords are quite strict and may not allow it. You don't want to sign a lease only to realize that you are not able to rent it out on Airbnb. Being completely transparent with your landlord is going to save you a lot of time and stress. You will also need to ensure that you have insurance and are protected for things like damages and injuries that take place on your property. This is part of the Aircover that Airbnb offers, but it is a good idea to get additional insurance to make sure you are completely covered.

If you have decided that rental arbitrage is something that you want to do, you need to start convincing your landlord to allow it. It is usually easier to find a property with a landlord that will allow subletting than to convince an existing contract to change. One thing to remember is that rental arbitrage is completely safe and legal, and if you follow the short-term rental laws in your state, county, or municipality, there is nothing for them to worry about.

Many landlords are under the false assumption that it is not allowed. If you come up with facts, then you'll have a better chance of succeeding. You should also show the landlord your strategy for how you plan to start an Airbnb. The risk is that they would want to do it themselves. That is why it is important to show why this is going to be beneficial for both of you since you will be handling all the work.

For example, you can let the landlord know that you will need to take much better care of the property than if you were living there. The goal is to make the most profit through Airbnb, which means giving your guests high-quality service. You will need to ensure that the amenities are working well and that your home is completely presentable, neat, and clean. On top of that, you can assure your landlord that they will be paid on time every month because you'll be running a lucrative business through the property. Since your income comes from renting out space, it will be easy for them to understand that you always have money to pay on time.

Your landlord may be concerned about the noise due to guests being in and out. They do not want to deal with this kind of disruption, so you need to reassure them that there will not be noise or parties happening in your Airbnb. There are ways that you can monitor this, such as by using noise tracking technology or stipulating there should be no noise past a certain time at the Airbnb. You will be able to enforce the rules with your guests to make sure they stick to them. Otherwise, there could be consequences.

You are presenting a strategy that will be a win-win for everyone involved. If they are already renting out their property on a long-term basis, they likely do not want to be as involved. Short-term rental means that you will need to be involved all the time to turn over the property and ensure the guests are happy. The landlord does not have to worry about any of this because you will be taking care of everything and making sure the property is well cared for.

While these innovative strategies can certainly boost your bookings and revenue, they can also introduce new risks to manage. In the next chapter, we will delve into risk management and policies to ensure your Airbnb business is not only profitable but also secure and sustainable in the long run.

12

RISK MANAGEMENT AND POLICIES

When you have an Airbnb, it is important to manage risk. There are many situations that can pop up that could cause you direct and financial harm. You don't want to be put in that position, as it can be demotivating. You can avoid most of it if you put the right measures in place.

SETTING HOUSE RULES AND SECURITY DEPOSITS

Let's first talk about house rules. This is mission-critical when you run an Airbnb. You want your guests to clearly understand what they are allowed and not allowed to do. What may be second nature to you might not be to others. Remember that people will be coming from all over the country and the world. There are different cultures and ways of doing things. If you leave things unexplained, there is no telling what will happen.

The type of rules you set will also determine the type of guests you attract. Every guest will be different, and it is important to consider why they are coming to stay with you. What might attract one guest to your Airbnb could repel another. It is also about respecting your guests. If your rules are too strict, then people will not want to stay with you. When someone is on vacation, they do not want to have a curfew, be unable to relax, or feel too restricted. You will need to filter your house rules so you stick to the ones that are actually important. If the list of rules is too long, they will likely not bother reading it. Then, they will not stick to the rules, which can cause problems. Your house rules should not be pages and pages long. Understand what matters and what you can just skip.

What you can do is set a few categories for your rules and then simply explain them within those categories. It will make it more manageable, and they will know the basics even if they do not read the full rules. Let's review a few categories and what can fall under each one. The first would be off-limits areas. There will be areas on your property that you might not want your guests snooping around. You would lock these, but it is also good to put a note in your rules. If the guests are bringing along pets or children, you might want to stipulate specific areas that should be restricted to them for their safety. You might also have storage areas, areas under construction, or general places you just don't want your guests in. Make a list of these areas under the heading of prohibited areas.

The next category would be smoking. It is up to you whether you allow smoking on your property. If you do allow it, it would be best to have designated smoking areas so your guests don't smoke anywhere they want to, which could ruin your furniture or worse. Remember that the smell of smoke is a turn-off for guests who do not smoke, so you do not want the smoke to stick to your furniture. Smoking areas should always be outside. Another category to consider is social events and parties. These can get out of hand very quickly and lead to injuries and damage to your property. If this is a big concern for you, then you can ban them entirely. You could also set rules and parameters if you do allow gatherings or parties.

Further categories would be extra guests and noise. An extra guest is an extra cost to you since they will be using the utilities and amenities. If extra guests are allowed, there should be an additional cost for them to stay the night. You can also set a limit on how many visitors can come by in a day. For noise, it will depend on where your Airbnb is situated. If it is in a remote area, it may be okay to be more easygoing. However, in a busy or residential area, there will be noise restrictions. You can set quiet hours if necessary and give general guidelines to keep the noise down.

The final category is trash. Every area and country has a different way of handling trash, which is why it is important to have guidelines and rules set out. There may be specific recycling rules in your area, so make sure your guests know about them and are able to follow them. You might also want to indicate that trash should not be left inside the property and should be properly disposed of in the designated trash containers.

There are plenty of other rule categories that you can highlight. It all depends on you and what you think is necessary. For example, specifying rules for appliance usage could be a good idea if you have specialized appliances that require specific handling.

You don't have to make these rules too long, as wordiness confuses people. Clear and concise instructions will serve you best.

Let's move on to security deposits. These are taken to cover any potential breakages or damages. The guest pays it to you, and you give it back to them in full if no damage has occurred. You cannot take a security deposit on the Airbnb platform without using API-connected software. This allows you to access the offline fee option on the platform. In other scenarios, you will not take a security deposit but instead request reimbursement for the damage caused by the guest. This will be done through the platform, and the guest's payment method will be charged. Then you will get the money for it.

Regarding damages and breakages, it is important to ask the guest first. Blindsiding them with a reimbursement request could end badly. You should always check the property as soon as you can after checkout. Make sure everything is there and accounted for. Having an inventory list for your property and all the rooms really helps. You will be able to keep track of all your items. You will be able to figure out if something is missing or broken quite quickly and can send in the reimbursement request. If you have taken a security deposit, you will check the room or home and then send the money back to them if there are no issues. If there was a problem, you could take the amount needed and send back the rest. It is a good idea to send the guest a message or email highlighting why you have issued the reimbursement or taken from the security deposit so that everyone is on the same page.

AIRBNB'S AIRCOVER

Insurance is an important part of every business, and even more so when you have a rental property. Accidents or issues can happen, and then you will need to foot the bill. This can be really expensive. Many businesses have gone down in situations like this. Most people simply do not have the money to cover large problems. Insurance steps in to help cover costs and protect you.

With Airbnb, every host has access to AirCover. It covers both liability and property damage and is automatically applied to every host. This means there are no extra steps involved. You can also get other types of insurance on your own, but AirCover will always apply. You will need to file a claim in order to get paid. The team at Airbnb will review this, and you will get a response in due course.

The property damage protection is called Airbnb Host Damage Protection. You get up to $3 million in protection for any damage caused by your guests, their visitors, or pets. The damages need to have taken place during the time between check-in and checkout. This protection also includes loss of income if the damage caused by the guest forces you to cancel future bookings. It is quite comprehensive, and it does get updated every so often. It is a good idea to go onto the Airbnb website and have a look at what it covers so you are fully prepared when the time comes. It is always best to submit a claim as soon as possible after the incident.

Getting additional insurance to cover the areas that AirCover does not cover might be a good idea. For example, AirCover does not cover damage caused by natural disasters. This means that if there were an earthquake and your property was damaged, you would have to pay cash for the repairs. In this case, it is best to get additional insurance so you are fully covered and don't have to worry about it.

Under AirCover, you also get Host Liability Insurance. This insurance program helps cover any legal responsibility you have as a host and also covers anyone who helps you, should there be some sort of issue on the property. This includes a guest or third-party getting hurt on your property or something of theirs being damaged or stolen during their stay. This insurance program gives you liability coverage for up to $1 million.

This type of insurance has been recently updated, and there are specific things it will cover. Just as with the previous type of insurance, it is important to have a look at the Airbnb website to see exactly what is covered and what is not. In general, any kind of bodily injury to the guest or other people on your property, or damage to their property while they are checked in at your Airbnb, will be covered. On top of that, it will cover damage that your guest has caused to a common area of a neighboring property. If damage has been caused but not by accident, this will not be covered. Any purposeful damage that is caused to your property by the guest is not covered. However, this is covered by the previous type of insurance.

When it comes to AirCover, it is important to understand exactly what is protected and covered. Many people get upset with AirCover simply because they do not understand the rules or what it will cover. In general, it works like many other types of insurance you can get from an insurance company. However, there are limits to what it does protect you from and what it doesn't. Remember that when you put in a claim for coverage, someone will go through the claim, do some research, and make sure that they reimburse you the necessary amount. This amount is decided based on many factors. This can mean that you don't get the results you want. For example, if you bought an antique lamp for $500, and the guest breaks it by accident, you may want to make a claim with AirCover. In your eyes, the lamp has appreciated in value, which means it has increased in value and is worth more now. However, the insurance team isn't going to take that into consideration. Instead, they will look at what you paid for the lamp and how long you've had it and then give you an amount based on that. You might only get $100 or $200 for the lamp. Sentimental value and potential value are not considered when it comes to almost any kind of insurance.

This is why knowing what to keep in your Airbnb and what you shouldn't is essential. Any sentimental or important items should be taken out, as you'll never receive the amount you believe is owed to you if something were to happen. At the end of the day, your guests probably don't even care about the antique lamp in the first place, so it's not going to add too much to your property. It is important to be smart with how you handle the layout of your property so that you can diminish the risk of accidents in the first place. Now that we have covered how to manage risks and safeguard your property, it's time to think bigger and go beyond the Airbnb platform.

13

EXPANDING YOUR REACH

Airbnb is a wonderful platform where you can get many benefits and tons of exposure. However, your rental property is a business first. Even if you want to be loyal to Airbnb, this might not be the best strategy for growing your business and seeking out more profit. Many different tools and platforms on the market could be really beneficial to you as you continue to grow. Considering these options could take your business to the next level.

LISTING ON MULTIPLE OTAS AND CREATING A DIRECT BOOKING SITE

Airbnb is definitely one of the larger property rental platforms. However, it is definitely not the only one. This means that just using Airbnb is costing you a few good opportunities. The goal is to reach as many people as possible so you can fill up your booking calendar. Many people prefer other platforms to

Airbnb. They could be loyal to their preference, and the only way to hook them in is to be where they are.

OTA stands for online travel agency. Using multiple OTAs has tons of benefits. You get the chance to maximize your income and increase the number of bookings you get. This is the goal for most people in this business. While there are all these benefits that you can access when you use multiple different sites to promote your property, there can also be a few challenges. It is important to understand these challenges so you can navigate through them and make sure that you aren't caught off guard. You will need a good plan in place to manage the bookings for multiple sites and not get overbooked and confused. If you do not manage this properly, it can lead to some very unhappy guests who will not want to stay with you again. The good news is that there are many strategies and tools. You can use them to navigate these problems so you can get the most out of your property rental.

Different sites may need different strategies in order to be successful. There are very different requirements across the channels, so knowing what you need from each is important. You will need to optimize your listing. The better your listings are, the more clicks you will get in there, and more guests will want to book your rooms. If you spend time optimizing your listing, then you don't have to keep doing this. Great photos, SEO, an amazing title, and a compelling description are all going to play a huge part in making your listing look desirable and credible.

You also have to be prepared for the specific challenges that come with using each of the sites. Not all of them are going to be built as well as you would wish. You might notice there are things you like about each one, as well as things you dislike. It's never going to be perfect, and that's why it's best to learn how to navigate the issues instead of simply giving up. One thing you will have to consider is that you will be paying a commission on each of the websites you use. Placing a listing is usually free, but almost all of them will charge a commission for every booking made. The amount will vary; some can be up to about 20 percent. You will have to keep in mind the different commission fees that will be taken out of your nightly rate. Navigating this can be a bit tough, but you must understand the financial aspects of hosting on various platforms such as Airbnb, Booking.com, Expedia, and VRBO.

Once you have decided that this is the route you want to take because of all the benefits, you can start looking into getting a channel manager. This is a great tool because it allows you to easily host on multiple sites. It allows you to do everything from one dashboard, so you don't have to keep switching between sites, which would make the process more complicated than it needs to be. You will be able to publish your listings on as many OTAs as you would like. Since everything is available on one dashboard, it is easy for you to keep track of things. That means there is almost no risk of double booking across the various sites. You will have a calendar that you can see, and it updates on all the sites, so if somebody has booked through site one, the same dates will not be available on-site two. You will need to pay a fee to use this type of tool, but it is really worth it if you are trying to scale your business. With that being said, you don't have to jump in right away. It is easy to manage your listings if you are only posting on one or two rental sites, in which case you might not need a channel manager. Once you get to a point where you want to accelerate the growth of your business, you can consider signing up with a channel manager.

A Direct Booking Site

A direct booking site is something slightly different from what we have discussed already. With this, you'll create your own website so potential guests can go there to find all the information they need about your rentals. You will be able to market your property as well as accept direct bookings from your website. Instead of your guests using Airbnb or another site to book with you, they just need to go onto your website, and in a few clicks, they will be booked. This is how hotels work. With hotels, you can go to the actual hotel site and book your room from there. They have direct booking sites. If you want to see how this looks or works, you can go onto any hotel website and have a look.

There are many benefits to doing it this way, and it doesn't mean you cannot use Airbnb or other rental sites either. When you have your own website, you have full control over what you put on it. It becomes part of your brand, and your guests are able to see what you stand for and the quality of service you provide. If you have multiple properties, this is a great way to cross-market. Someone who had an amazing time staying at one location might want to book at another location as well. All they have to do is go onto the website and see all the different locations that you have properties in. They would expect the exact same type of service and quality each time they stay with you.

You can also use your website as a marketing tool because you get to use SEO, which helps people find you. You can use techniques such as creating blogs, newsletters, and social media to help build your brand through your website. You can put as much information as you want about your property and business on your website. When people search the internet, they will put in a few keywords. If you have these keywords on your website, you'll have a higher likelihood of showing up on the first or second page of the search results. This means that anyone looking for a property to stay in that is similar to yours would be able to find it easily.

Another benefit is that you do not have to worry about booking fees. With all other sites you post a listing on, you have to consider the commission you owe them. Since this is your own site, it's not a concern. All the money that is paid to you goes directly into your pocket. You can end up saving quite a bit of money this way.

You can hire somebody to create the website for you, but there are easy ways to do it using a website hosting provider. Typically, they will offer you all the support you need to easily build your website. You get to design it the way you want to, and you can get support as you need it. There are a few things that you have to ensure that you have. One of the most important things is a secure payment gateway. Whenever you purchase something online, you are usually redirected to a secure payment gateway. This ensures that both parties are protected, and that the money is transferred from one bank to another safely. It is also a good idea to make sure that your website is mobile-friendly because most people use the internet on their mobile phones. If the site is too difficult to navigate on a mobile device, they will probably click out and look for something else.

USING SOCIAL MEDIA FOR MARKETING

Social media is another powerful marketing tool at your disposal. Social media is also completely free. This means you can build your brand and market yourself without any monetary investment. With that being said, as you get more comfortable on social media, you can start looking at paid options that can boost your marketing strategy. Almost all successful businesses are on social media. That is because they all recognize how powerful a tool it is. Most people spend at least a few hours on social media every single day. Using it means that you get the attention of people you may not be able to connect with simply through a website or various property rental platforms.

There are different requirements that come with each type of social media platform. This means you'll need a different strategy for each one. On top of that, each social media platform shows a different kind of content and has different audiences. If you stick to only one type of social media, then you will only target a specific type of person. However, you want your reach to be as wide as possible. The good news is you can repurpose content and use it across multiple social media platforms. You might need to make a few tweaks here and there, but it is quite simple to post on various platforms.

When running social media pages for your business, you must ensure you have a plan. Pages that post consistently are the ones that get the most traction and attention. It also gives you a sense of credibility when you are constantly posting on social media. It can get overwhelming to post all the time, so one of the best things you can do is take some time to create lots of content. You can create posts and images and then simply save them as drafts. Then, once or twice a week, you can post on your social media channels. This should only take a few seconds, so it doesn't take much of your day. The best times to post are usually during the day on a workday. The truth is that there are far fewer people on social media on the weekend because everybody is busy doing things with their friends and family. People are more likely to be on social media during lunch hours and after work, which means your posts will get more views when you post at those times.

Facebook

Facebook is the original social media platform that people remember. Sure, there were definitely other social media platforms before Facebook, but Facebook has stood the test of time and continues to stand strong over the years. You can post your

Airbnb listings on Facebook to generate more traction. You can easily connect your Facebook account to Airbnb, so it is easy to post your listings on Facebook. All you will need to do is go onto your Airbnb account and click on a feature called social accounts. Here, you can easily connect your Facebook account and be walked through all the steps to create a secure connection. You can also disconnect your account in the same manner if you find you no longer want it.

The first thing you want to do is create a business page for your Airbnb on Facebook. You can share information on your personal page, but that means the only people you'll be reaching are your direct friends and family. You want to reach a wider audience, so creating a dedicated page will help you do that. If you make a business page, you can also share that page on your personal social media if you want to. Having a social media page for your Airbnb means that you put forward a sense of professionalism to your potential guests. It is straightforward to set up a page. All you have to do is click "Create a page" and then follow the instructions.

Speaking about Facebook, I have created a Facebook group for Airbnb hosts to connect, share their experiences, and learn. There is so much to learn, and you can pick up some great tips from others. If you would like to join, here are the details:

Name: Airbnb Host Community

URL: www.facebook.com/groups/airbnbhostcommunity

QR Code:

Instagram

Instagram and Facebook are linked social media platforms. This means whatever you post on Instagram, you can also immediately post the same thing on Facebook. All you have to do is link the profiles, and you are good to go. That's a great advantage, as it requires minimal effort on your part. Instagram is a photo-based social media platform. Make sure you are taking high-quality pictures that you can post. You can then give a little description at the bottom and click "Share."

The great thing about a platform run with pictures is that there is a never-ending supply of content. You can give people a tour of your house, show your guests having a good time, and advertise other businesses in the area. The options are basically endless. With the new update to Instagram, you can also post video content in the form of reels. These get quite a lot of visibility if you can create content that people want to engage with. You can use the same content that you create on TikTok to post to your Instagram reel, so you're not doing double the work. We will talk about TikTok shortly.

LinkedIn

LinkedIn is a professional networking site that can also be used to market your Airbnb. Since LinkedIn is a more professional network, it is definitely more trusted, and you are more credible when you have a LinkedIn profile. It can also help you connect with people who are in the same industry as you. This can help you be part of a community where you can share ideas and grow your business in a completely different way. You can connect with other businesses that inspire you and that you want to follow. This helps you get other ideas so you can continue learning and becoming better in your field. While this may not be a strictly Airbnb marketing or social media platform, you can use it to grow your brand and connect with people who can help you build your business in the future.

TikTok

TikTok is one of the newer social media platforms, but it has grown so fast in its 7 years of existence that it is actually crazy.

With TikTok, you can post short-form video content. This takes a little more work than posting photos or status updates on other social media platforms. However, TikTok has the unique ability to make things go viral. If one of your posts goes viral, it means that thousands or even millions of people will see it. This is great exposure for your business. And don't worry, TikTok is not just for teenagers; there are millions of adults who are also on the platform.

When you have a vacation rental, you have access to travel content. Travel content is some of the most popular and watched content on TikTok. The younger and even the older generations love to travel and see various locations. If you are able to break into the niche market on TikTok, you will quickly gain a lot of traction and possibly go viral. It does take a bit of practice to learn what kinds of videos get the most views. However, a quick hack is to look at the songs that are the most popular on TikTok. If you use these songs and put them in the background of your TikTok posts, then you will have a higher chance of going viral and being seen. You can also post your TikTok videos on Instagram reels, which means you get more use out of them.

X (Twitter)

X, which was formerly known as Twitter, is another platform that you can use to market yourself on social media. The landscape has changed slightly since Elon Musk took over. There are a lot of changes taking place with the platform, which means that it may change the way brands use it to market themselves. With this platform, you will need to post short text content. This allows you to share information and your opinions on various aspects. You can post tips and tricks for traveling and staying at Airbnbs. This way, the content you post is valuable to a wide audience, and you have a higher chance of people connecting with it. You can also post pictures and videos onto the platform, so you're not just limited to text. However, it is a good idea to always include some sort of text, even if you post a video or pictures, since this is a text-based platform.

BECOMING A CO-HOST FOR OTHER AIRBNB OWNERS

Perhaps you are at a point in life where you cannot afford a property to post on Airbnb on your own. There is another option: You can become an Airbnb Co-Host. The owner of the Airbnb can decide what you have access to and can manage your payouts as well. Many Airbnb hosts do not have the time to do the work, which is why they would want a Co-Host to come in and handle most of the work for them. You will then get paid through the Airbnb platform because the host will decide on the payment split that works best for them. You can definitely negotiate if you need to.

It is important to remember that Co-Hosting is quite a bit of work. The reason you are becoming a Co-Host is to handle all the nitty-gritty aspects of renting an Airbnb. Each host is going to be completely different, so it is important to find out what they expect from you when you are Co-Hosting for them. If they give you full access to their Airbnb platform, it means that you will have access to the calendar, listings, messages, and transaction history. There are other options that allow you much less access. Some of you will only have access to the calendar; others will have access to the calendar and can message guests.

You will need to have a conversation with the host of the property so you understand exactly what your tasks will be. It is a good idea to create a resume for yourself so you can start applying for these jobs. Becoming a Co-Host is a great way to understand what is required to run your own Airbnb. It gets you a foot in the door so you can gain experience for when you host your very own property. You also get additional income from this job, which you can put towards saving for a property. In most cases, this can be a part-time job, depending on how many properties the owner has and how much work they want you to put in.

With all of this being said, you could also get a Co-Host on board for your Airbnb. If you find the work too much for you to handle, you can get a friend, family member, or someone else to become a Co-Host on the platform for you. It may make things a lot more manageable, and you will have a lot more free time and not have to worry about messaging guests and organizing the calendars.

We've explored some innovative ways to expand your reach and boost your income. But with increased scale comes increased complexity. In the next chapter, we'll delve into selecting the right management tools to help streamline operations, save time, and reduce stress.

14

CHOOSING THE RIGHT TOOLS FOR MANAGEMENT

Many people are getting into Airbnb and vacation rentals because they are so profitable. The industry is absolutely booming. However, this means there is way more competition now than ever before. In order to set yourself apart from the rest, it is beneficial to look into technology-based tools. Most property managers tend to rely on these tools to help them become more effective in their jobs. Knowing which tools to use can simplify the process and make you much more productive. This results in more income and easier management of your property.

PMS AND PRICING MANAGERS

In a previous chapter, we mentioned channel managers. These tools help you manage your listings on various platforms from one dashboard. In this section, we will be talking about two other tools that could be incredibly useful in your Airbnb journey. The first one is Property Management Software (PMS).

Making sure your property is up to standard can be a difficult task. It is even more so when you have multiple properties to worry about. Using property management software makes things so much easier to keep track of. It also allows you to incorporate automation into your property management. You'll get to manage things like maintenance tasks, revenue, guest communication, and channels, all wrapped up in one box.

Maintenance management is one of the most important things when it comes to running your own Airbnb. This is something that many people forget to do because it's not at the top of their priority list. However, this results in a loss of income when something happens that needs to be repaired. This is not something you want to happen to you, so having a maintenance schedule is so important. When you have proper maintenance management software, you'll be reminded to do various maintenance tasks that directly impact the quality of your Airbnb. It allows you to streamline your tasks and automatically assign tasks to different people and vendors. This means you know the schedules are being kept and that your property is well cared for.

Another important feature of property management software is that you get access to accounting features. Money management is one of the most important things to consider when running your own business. You need to pay for things, as well as make sure you have a good profit margin. Doing this without proper software can be really difficult, especially when you have multiple properties and sources of income to consider. An accounting system will allow you to have everything in one place so you can easily see it and work from there. Your financial decisions will be much more balanced, and you can make sure you have enough money for important things.

This leads us to pricing managers, which are great tools when running an Airbnb or any vacation rental. This tool helps you automatically price your vacation rentals to optimize your pricing strategies. This way, you can make the most money with the least amount of effort. It will take into account various metrics as it works out the ideal pricing strategy for you. So many programs have this feature; some of the best include Beyond, Wheelhouse, and PriceLabs. These can be fully integrated into most property management software, and that's why it is important to choose a good one.

Here are some PMS to consider:

- Avantio
- Hostaway
- Hospitable
- Hosthub
- Hostfully
- iGMS
- Guesty
- Lodgify
- OwnerRez
- Uplisting
- Zeevou

It is always important to do your own research and make sure you have picked the one that's going to work best for you. If you want to read and compare reviews, you can go to www.-capterra.com. You also have to consider the fees that come with using this technology and pick one that suits your current budget. You can always make changes later on when you have different needs. Plus, so many new types of technology keep coming on the market that you can consider.

INSTANT BOOK AND SMART PRICING

Instant Book and Smart Pricing are tools that are available on Airbnb. You can use them to help improve your property management and ensure you are getting the most out of the platform. Airbnb allows its hosts access to amazing tools that can really assist in their profitability. However, there are always advantages and drawbacks when it comes to this type of thing. You will need to decide for yourself whether these options are good for you, or if you need to seek out something else.

Let's start by talking about the Instant Book function. We have already mentioned this briefly in a previous chapter. With Instant Book, your guests can simply click and book without you confirming first. This is an amazing feature for last-minute bookings because it gives the guests security that they will have a place to stay when they book with you, and you don't have to worry about confirming before then. Not only that, but there is a filter guests can use to filter out properties that do not use Instant Book. This means your pool of potential guests will be smaller when you do not use this function.

As a host, you can receive same-day bookings when this feature is on. Someone can easily book a stay at your accommodation on the day they are going to arrive. You are able to specify when same-day and instant bookings are no longer available for that day. This means you can set a cutoff time, which makes it easier to manage. If you do not want to use same-day bookings, you can still use the Instant Book function; however, you will need to add an advance notice to your Airbnb listing. If you are using same-day booking, you may want to consider a self-check-in process so you do not have to be there to check your guests in. It'll make things a lot easier for you, and you'll still have flexibility.

Smart Pricing is another tool you can use to optimize your pricing strategy on the Airbnb platform. If you struggle with pricing, then this could be a useful tool. The tool evaluates relevant data from the property listings on Airbnb and then prices your property accordingly. It will automatically update the price depending on what is going on in the current rental market. This means if your area is in demand, you can increase the price to make more profit, and if there is a slow month, you can lower the price to still attract travelers who want a cheaper option.

It is important to note that Airbnb's smart pricing tends to set the price too low. This means you will end up losing income even though pricing is much easier to manage using the system. If this is your first time on the Airbnb platform and your property is new to the platform, then using this tool is great because you can attract people at a lower price. However, once you have gained some credibility on the platform, you may no longer want to use the smart pricing tool. There are a lot of gaps in this technology, so it is important to recognize that. It is definitely not one of the best pricing tools on the market. However, the better ones tend to be slightly more expensive. You will just need to weigh the pros and cons of using this technology versus another one. On top of that, you could manually do your own pricing and work on your pricing strategy. With all that being said, Smart Pricing is a good option for those just getting started with their Airbnb. Just make sure to monitor and check so that you know when it is time to move on to something different so you can make more profit.

This brings us to the end of our journey through the intricacies of running a successful Airbnb business. However, this is just the beginning of your own journey. In the book's conclusion, we will review our journey together, summarize key takeaways, and, most importantly, talk about your next steps to make your Airbnb business not just survive but thrive.

Help Another Airbnb Owner Out

As a fellow Airbnb owner, you know how difficult it can be when you're first getting started – and this is your chance to make the road a little easier for someone else.

Simply by sharing your honest opinion of this book and a little about your own experience, you'll show new readers where they can find the guidance they're looking for to see success with their property listing.

Thank you for your support. I wish you the best of luck with your business.

Scan the QR code below

CONCLUSION

A great way to make a huge amount of money in the rental industry is by using effective strategies. There are so many tactics to increase your profitability and ensure your business is as successful as possible. Whether you have just started out on your Airbnb journey or you have been in the industry for quite a while, the tools you have learned will help you increase profitability and make sure you are as productive as possible.

Even implementing one or two of the things you have learned in this book will greatly help you increase your bookings. Can you imagine what would happen if you used them all? I'm not suggesting that you jump in and try to do too much at once. It is usually best to try one thing at a time so you can implement it properly before moving on to the next. The truth is that many of these tactics require time and money. You will need to plan in order to implement them properly. That way, you can ensure you are getting the most out of the tools and tricks you have learned.

As you turn the final page of this book, you're not just closing a chapter—you're opening the door to a new era of growth. Take the first step, the next, and the one after that. Ponder the area you want to improve upon, and then create a step-by-step plan to implement your decision. Start taking actionable steps toward your goal. At the end of the day, if you do not practice what you have learned, then it won't do anything for you. Taking the right steps will always yield the best results.

I wrote another book, *How to Set Up and Run a Successful Airbnb Business: Outearn Your Competition with Skyrocketing Rental Income and Leave Your 9 to 5 Job Even If You Are an Absolute Beginner.* I started this book with a powerful quote, and I will use this same quote to sign off this book.

"The longer you're not taking action, the more money you're losing."

— CARRIE WILKERSON

REFERENCES

1Angel17. (2022, November 11). *Switch to LTR?* Reddit. https://www.reddit.com/r/realestateinvesting/comments/ys49hd/switch_to_ltr

6 creative ways to collaborate with local businesses at your airbnb. (2021, August 24). Mama Mode. https://mammamode.com/6-creative-ways-to-collaborate-with-local-businesses-at-your-airbnb/

7 steps to an unbeatable airbnb pricing strategy. (2023, February). Guest Ready. https://www.guestready.com/blog/airbnb-pricing-strategy-tips/

10 key benefits of market research. (2018, June 26). Turquoise. https://thinkturquoise.com/blog/market-research/10-key-benefits-of-market-research/

16 actionable ways to increase bookings during off season. (2022, August 14). Hostfully. https://www.hostfully.com/blog/more-bookings-airbnb-off-season/

70 relevant analytics statistics: 2021/2022 market share analysis & data. (2019, October 7). Finances Online. https://financesonline.com/relevant-analytics-statistics/

A step-by-step guide to pricing your place on airbnb. (n.d.). Padlifter. https://padlifter.com/free-tips-and-resources/pricing/a-step-by-step-guide-to-pricing-your-place-on-airbnb/

Airbnb automated messages: A guide to guest communication. (2020, October 23). Host Tools. https://hosttools.com/blog/short-term-rental-automation/airbnb-automated-messages/

Airbnb cleaning fee: Everything you need to know. (2023, February 2). Hospitable. https://hospitable.com/airbnb-cleaning-fees-heres-everything-you-need-to-know/

Airbnb cleaning fee: Facts and figures you should know. (2022, December 28). IGMS. https://www.igms.com/airbnb-cleaning-fee/

Airbnb co-host: Beginner's guide. (2023, May 9). Hospitable. https://hospitable.com/airbnb-co-host/

Airbnb house rules: Best examples and free template. (n.d.). Lodgify. https://www.lodgify.com/guides/airbnb-house-rules/

Airbnb instant book: Useful information for hosts. (n.d.). Lodgify. https://www.lodgify.com/guides/airbnb/instant-book/

REFERENCES

Airbnb pricing strategies to boost your profit [master class summary]. (2020, February 3). IGMS. https://www.igms.com/airbnb-pricing/

Airbnb rental arbitrage [and how to succeed at it]. (2021, November 17). Hostfully. https://www.hostfully.com/blog/airbnb-rental-arbitrage/

Airbnb self check-in: 5 steps to automating the check-in process. (2021, February 23). Host Tools. https://hosttools.com/blog/short-term-rental-automation/airbnb-self-check-in/

Airbnb self-check-in: How it works and how to set it up. (2021, January 29). IGMS. https://www.igms.com/airbnb-self-check-in/

Airbnb smart pricing – should you use it? (2023, March 29). Floorspace. https://www.getfloorspace.com/airbnb-smart-pricing/

Airbnb tools: The complete list (2021 update). (2020, July 3). Airbnb Smart. https://airbnbsmart.com/airbnb-tools/

Amadebai, E. (2020, December 10). *13 reasons why data is important in decision making*. Analytics for Decisions. https://www.analyticsfordecisions.com/data-is-important-in-decision-making/

An in-depth guide to airbnb smart pricing [+ alternatives]. (2022, June 5). Hostfully. https://www.hostfully.com/blog/airbnb-smart-pricing-and-alternatives/

Analytics comes of age. (2018). In McKinsey Analytics. https://www.mckinsey.com/~/media/McKinsey/Business%20Functions/McKinsey%20Analytics/Our%20Insights/Analytics%20comes%20of%20age/Analytics-comes-of-age.ashx

Average airbnb prices by city [2022]. (2022). AllTheRooms. https://www.alltherooms.com/resources/articles/average-airbnb-prices-by-city/

Average daily rate (ADR) vacation rental metrics. (2018, November 26). AirDNA. https://www.airdna.co/blog/vacation-rental-metrics-adr

Average daily rate (ADR) vacation rental metrics | ADR calculation. (2018, November 26). AirDNA. https://www.airdna.co/blog/vacation-rental-metrics-adr

Booking lead time | vacation rental metrics. (2019, February 2). AirDNA - Short-Term Vacation Rental Data and Analytics. https://www.airdna.co/blog/vacation-rental-metrics-booking-lead-time

Caravitis, A. (n.d.). *How to build a direct booking website for vacation rentals for under $100*. Hosthub. https://www.hosthub.com/guides/how-to-create-your-own-direct-booking-website/

Cariaga, V. (2023, July 9). *Housing market 2023: Viral tweet says "airbnb collapse is real" — is now the time to buy a home?* Yahoo. https://finance.yahoo.com/news/housing-market-2023-viral-tweet-113009741.html?

Channel manager partners. (n.d.). Airbnb. https://www.airbnb.com/help/article/3304

Choose the right cancellation policy for you. (2020, February 5). Airbnb. https://www.airbnb.com/resources/hosting-homes/a/choose-the-right-cancellation-policy-for-you-19

Clark, R. (2021, June 28). *How to advertise your airbnb on facebook in 7 easy steps.* Lodgify. https://www.lodgify.com/blog/advertise-airbnb-facebook/

Consider your area and circumstances when pricing. (2023, May 25). Airbnb. https://www.airbnb.com/resources/hosting-homes/a/consider-your-area-and-circumstances-when-pricing-589

Dasgupta, N. (2023, July 7). *Importance of improving your quality on your airbnb listing featured.* Staah. https://blog.staah.com/featured/importance-of-improving-your-quality-on-your-airbnb-listing

Dynamic pricing strategy: Definition, types, benefits & examples. (n.d.). Paddle. https://www.paddle.com/resources/dynamic-pricing-model

Elon musk quotes. (n.d.). BrainyQuote. https://www.brainyquote.com/quotes/elon_musk_567298

Everything you need to know about the airbnb search algorithm. (n.d.). Hostaway. https://www.hostaway.com/airbnb-search-algorithm/

Freeze, P. (2022, September 20). *How to encourage repeat guests in your vacation rental.* Bay Property Management Group. https://www.baymgmtgroup.com/blog/how-to-encourage-repeat-guests-in-your-vacation-rental/

Fuchs, J. (2022, July 9). *Dynamic pricing: The complete guide.* Blog.hubspot.com. https://blog.hubspot.com/sales/dynamic-pricing#f

Hollander, J. (2023, February 16). *The 6 best airbnb pricing tools in 2023.* Hotel Tech Report. https://hoteltechreport.com/news/airbnb-pricing-tools

How do rule-sets work? (n.d.). Airbnb Help Centre. https://www.airbnb.com/help/article/2061

How does airbnb dynamic pricing drive revenue growth? (2021, May 21). IGMS. https://www.igms.com/dynamic-pricing-airbnb/

How does the airbnb cancellation policy work? (2019, March 29). Medium. https://medium.com/@airgms/how-does-the-airbnb-cancellation-policy-work-e5333b9541b2

How hosts on airbnb help support small businesses. (2020, November 25). Airbnb

Newsroom. https://news.airbnb.com/how-hosts-on-airbnb-help-support-small-businesses/

How smart is airbnb smart pricing and should you be using it? (2021, March 19). IGMS. https://www.igms.com/airbnb-smart-pricing/

How to automate airbnb cleaning: 6 simple tips for hosts. (n.d.). Turno. https://turno.com/automate-airbnb-cleaning/

How to charge extra fees for services: A community help guide. (2016, June 3). Airbnb Community Center. https://community.withairbnb.com/t5/Help-with-your-business/How-to-Charge-Extra-Fees-for-Services-A-Community-Help-Guide/td-p/101736

How to get good reviews on airbnb | 5-star vacation rental reviews. (n.d.). Vacasa. https://www.vacasa.com/homeowner-guides/how-to-get-good-reviews-airbnb

How to get more airbnb bookings during the off-season. (2023, January 10). Hospitable. https://hospitable.com/get-airbnb-bookings-during-off-season/

How to prepare your airbnb for peak season. (2023, May 12). AirDNA. https://www.airdna.co/blog/how-to-prepare-your-airbnb-for-peak-season

How to set a pricing strategy. (2020, December 1). Airbnb. https://www.airbnb.com/resources/hosting-homes/a/how-to-set-a-pricing-strategy-15

How to set up an effective listing page. (2020, November 18). Airbnb. https://www.airbnb.com/resources/hosting-homes/a/how-to-set-up-an-effective-listing-page-12

How to supercharge your airbnb listing with instagram. (2019, October 14). Guest-Ready. https://www.guestready.com/blog/airbnb-hosts-instagram/

How to switch from entire home to private room. (2018, February 12). Community.withairbnb.com. https://community.withairbnb.com/t5/Hosting/How-to-switch-from-entire-home-to-private-room/td-p/614322

How to turn your short-term rental properties into pet friendly paradises. (n.d.). Guesty. https://www.guesty.com/guide/turn-your-short-term-rental-properties-into-pet-friendly-paradises/

How to use social media to advertise airbnb property. (2021, November 24). Hosty. https://www.hostyapp.com/social-media-and-airbnb-property/

InternationalPirate. (2022, February 3). *Any positive experiences with "aircover?"* Reddit. https://www.reddit.com/r/AirBnB/comments/sjusx2/any_positive_experiences_with_aircover/

Is linkedin helpful for your vacation rental? (n.d.). Hostaway. https://www.hostaway.com/linkedin-for-your-vacation-rental/

Johnson, D. (2020, February 24). *Why and how to do market research for your vacation rental.* Simple Vacation Rental Management Software. https://your.rentals/blog/market-research-for-your-short-term-rental-business/

Kemmis, S. (2022, May 3). *Unpopular opinion: Airbnb has become terrible.* NerdWallet. https://www.nerdwallet.com/article/travel/airbnb-terrible

Krones, T. (2023). *What is an orphan period pricing rule?* Host Tools Help Center. https://help.hosttools.com/en/articles/5105363-what-is-an-orphan-period-pricing-rule

Lauzon, A. (2022, November 29). *How to research an airbnb market and quickly find a good place to buy rental property.* Mashvisor Real Estate Blog. https://www.mashvisor.com/blog/how-to-research-airbnb-market/

Leavy, J. (2020, June 17). *How to deal with bad airbnb guests (5 tips).* AirHost Academy. https://airhostacademy.com/how-to-deal-with-bad-airbnb-guests/

McClymont, A. (2023, June 19). *Boost your airbnb success with strategic market research: Choose the perfect property to maximize....* Medium. https://medium.com/@astrid.mcclymont/how-to-choose-the-most-profitable-airbnb-property-through-market-research-b9f95a63fc61

Must-Have airbnb tools & apps. (n.d.). Hostaway. https://www.hostaway.com/must-have-airbnb-tools-and-apps/

NoPressureLife. (2021, August 9). *All the automation ideas. give me some time back!* Reddit. https://www.reddit.com/r/airbnb_hosts/comments/p0q9w9/all_the_automation_ideas_give_me_some_time_back/

Peña, R. (2022, June 25). *The ultimate guide: How to find rental arbitrage properties.* Airbtics | Airbnb Analytics. https://airbtics.com/how-to-find-rental-arbitrage-properties/

Ribbers, J. (2019, December 10). *7 ways to boost your bottom line with airbnb add-on services.* Get Paid for Your Pad. https://getpaidforyourpad.com/blog/additional-revenue-airbnb/

Rodriguez, A. (2022, February 20). *How to find out the airbnb demand in my area.* Mashvisor Real Estate Blog. https://www.mashvisor.com/blog/airbnb-demand-in-my-area/

Rogers, C. (2022, August 9). *Off-Season airbnb tips for higher bookings.* DPGO. https://www.dpgo.com/go/off-season-airbnb-tips-for-higher-bookings/

Scott, R. (2023, May 19). *Airbnb data and analytics to optimize your listing.* Beyond

Pricing. https://www.beyondpricing.com/blog/airbnb-data-and-analytics-to-optimize-your-listing

Security deposits. (n.d.). Airbnb. https://www.airbnb.com/help/article/140

Seven ways airbnb hosts can increase revenues with a directory website. (2023, February 24). GeoDirectory. https://wpgeodirectory.com/seven-ways-airbnb-hosts-can-increase-revenues-with-a-directory-website/

Shirshikov, D. (2023, April 19). *Airbnb occupancy rate: What to expect for your property.* Awning. https://awning.com/post/airbnb-occupancy-rate

Should you list your vacation rental on multiple channels? Or stick to airbnb? (n.d.). Hostaway. https://www.hostaway.com/should-you-list-your-vacation-rental-on-multiple-channels/

Six ways that short-term vacation rentals are impacting communities. (2017, April 15). Granicus. https://granicus.com/blog/six-ways-that-short-term-vacation-rentals-are-impacting-communities/

Static vs. dynamic marketplace pricing - how to choose. (2022, July 1). StoreAutomator. https://www.storeautomator.com/blog/static-vs-dynamic-marketplace-pricing-how-to-choose/

Steve jobs quotes. (n.d.). BrainyQuote. https://www.brainyquote.com/quotes/steve_jobs_173474

Succeed at airbnb long-term rentals: Strategy and tips. (n.d.). Hostfully. https://www.hostfully.com/blog/airbnb-long-term-rentals/

Tamplin, T. (2022, May 2). *What is a financial strategy? | importance, types, and steps.* Finance Strategists. https://www.financestrategists.com/financial-advisor/financial-plan/financial-strategy/

The advantages of outsourcing airbnb cleaning to a professional service in toronto. (2023, January 25). UpMaid. https://www.upmaid.com/the-advantages-of-outsourcing-airbnb-cleaning-to-a-professional-service-in-toronto/

The basics of communicating with guests. (2020, January 8). Airbnb. https://www.airbnb.com/resources/hosting-homes/a/the-basics-of-communicating-with-guests-33

The best airbnb pricing tools in 2022 - maximize your profits with dynamic pricing. (n.d.). Floorspace. https://www.getfloorspace.com/best-airbnb-pricing-tools/

The importance of airbnb cleaning: Why a clean property is essential for providing a positive guest experience. (2023, January 3). Turnify. https://www.turnify.com/the-importance-of-airbnb-cleaning-why-a-clean-property-is-essential-for-providing-a-positive-guest-experience/

TikTok for vacation rentals: Fad or marketing opportunity? (2021, June 24). Rentals United. https://rentalsunited.com/blog/tiktok-marketing-vacation-rentals/

Top 5 property management software for airbnb [2023 guide]. (2022, September 21). Door Loop. https://www.doorloop.com/blog/property-management-software-for-airbnb

Understanding airbnb market research. (2023, June 22). IGMS. https://www.igms.com/understanding-airbnb-market-research-for-vacation-rental-hosts-a-guide-to-success/

Understanding response rate and acceptance rate. (2021, April 21). Airbnb. https://www.airbnb.com/resources/hosting-homes/a/understanding-response-rate-and-acceptance-rate-86

Understanding your market. (2023, May 25). Lloyds Bank. https://www.lloydsbank.com/business/resource-centre/business-guides/understanding-your-market.html

Using social media to market your airbnb. (n.d.). Hostaway. https://www.hostaway.com/using-social-media-to-market-your-airbnb/

van Eyk, L. (n.d.). *A landlord's guide to mid-term rentals.* Steadily. https://www.steadily.com/blog/guide-to-mid-term-rentals

Wahi, U. (2022, December 13). *How to craft authentic guest experiences by partnering with local businesses | rental scale-up.* Rental Scale Up. https://www.rentalscaleup.com/how-to-craft-authentic-guest-experiences-by-partnering-with-local-businesses/

Welcoming guests in person vs self check in - will it impact ratings? (2018, May 11). Airhostsforum. https://airhostsforum.com/t/welcoming-guests-in-person-vs-self-check-in-will-it-impact-ratings/22558

What airbnb aircover is and how it works. (n.d.). Hostaway. https://www.hostaway.com/airbnb-aircover/

What are short term rentals? (n.d.). Lodgify. https://www.lodgify.com/guides/business/short-term/

What is airbnb superhost status and is it worth getting? (2021, March 15). IGMS. https://www.igms.com/airbnb-superhost/

What is RevPAR? (2019). STR. https://str.com/data-insights-blog/what-is-revpar

What is the average airbnb pet fee? What is reasonable? (2023, April 15). BnB Facts. https://bnbfacts.com/what-is-the-average-airbnb-pet-fee-what-is-reasonable/

What to do when you receive a bad review on airbnb. (2014, March 21). Guesty. https://www.guesty.com/blog/handle-getting-bad-review/

Why you NEED airbnb dynamic pricing - expert tips. (2015, June 16). LearnBNB. https://learnbnb.com/airbnb-supply-demand-dynamic-airbnb-pricing/

Woodward, M. (2022, August 16). *Airbnb statistics [2023]: User & market growth data.* Search Logistics. https://www.searchlogistics.com/learn/statistics/airbnb-statistics/

Your airbnb pricing strategy SUCKS. (2014, August 2). LearnBNB.com. https://learnbnb.com/airbnb-pricing-strategy-sucks/

Image References

Distel, A. (2019, July 24). *Person using laptop and smartphone* [Image]. Unsplash. https://unsplash.com/photos/tLZhFRLj6nY

Dole777. (2020, January 24). *iPhone with social media icons* [Image]. Unsplash. https://unsplash.com/photos/EQSPI11rf68

Fauxels. (n.d.). *Group of Friends Making Toast* [Image]. Pexels. https://www.pexels.com/photo/group-of-friends-making-toast-3184193/

Fewings, B. (2018, August 8). *Colorful welcome sign* [Image]. Unsplash. https://unsplash.com/photos/6wAGwpsXHE0

Firmbee. (2015, May 29). *Person writing on paper* [Image]. Unsplash. https://unsplash.com/photos/gcsNOsPEXfs

Forseck, R. (2020, September 10). *Black and white dog laying on dog bed* [Image]. Unsplash. https://unsplash.com/photos/Mlrc9NwoZFk

PhotoMIX Company. (2016, Mar 17). *Documents on Wooden Surface* [Image]. Pexels. https://www.pexels.com/photo/documents-on-wooden-surface-95916/

Muza, C. (2016, April 17). *Laptop on table* [Image]. Unsplash. https://unsplash.com/photos/hpjSkU2UYSU

Trovato, G. (2023, June 8). *Woman vacuuming ottoman* [Image]. Unsplash. https://unsplash.com/photos/5TXz228u4eo

ABOUT THE AUTHOR

Frank Eberstadt is an accommodation manager and the author of *How to Set Up and Run a Successful Airbnb Business* & *How to Unleash Your Airbnb's Full Potential*.

His books address property management and business growth in Airbnb, guiding readers to seek and capitalize on opportunities in the market, nurturing successful businesses on the way.

Frank is the accommodation manager for an investment group operating hotels and motels in Australia. He has established his own successful Airbnb business, and has grown his portfolio to six properties. Frank began his first Airbnb business from the ground up and knows how hard it can be to break into property listings and attract guests. Using his extensive experience in the accommodation industry, his aim is to lay out a clear, step-by-step path that even complete newbies can follow to success.

Frank's interest in vacation property stems from his many years traveling as a solo backpacker, something he now does with his family. These two very different traveling experiences have fed into his awareness of what makes a successful vacation rental, and have been key to his success as an Airbnb business owner.

Frank still loves to travel, and enjoys surfing, but more than anything, he loves to spend quality time with his family, no matter where their adventures take them.